Running Your Own Wine Bar

running your own
WINE BAR

Judy Ridgway

**THE
KOGAN PAGE**
Working for Yourself
SERIES

Acknowledgements

I would like to say a heartfelt thank-you to all the wine bar owners who took time out to answer all my many questions, but particular thanks are due to David Belford of Coolings in Exeter, Allan and Pam Diamond of Tempters in Middlewich, Richard Gale of Gales in Llangollen, Robin Hotton of the Grapevine in Crediton, Steve Jones of the Pipe of Port in Southend, David Nichols of Bubbles in Mayfair, Nigel Ravenshill of Wheels in Bideford, Judith and Michael Rose of Boos in Marylebone and James Walker of Wildes in Leamington Spa. Thanks are also due to Dick Johnston, Managing Director of Securit Services Ltd, Duncan Ritchie, Sales Director of Grants Wine and Spirit Merchants, and my brother Brian Ridgway, Operations Director of the Thistle Group of Hotels, for their invaluable specialist advice.

Judy Ridgway
November 1983

First published in Great Britain in 1984
by Kogan Page Limited
120 Pentonville Road
London N1 9JN

British Library Cataloguing in Publication Data

Ridgway, Judy
  Running your own wine bar.
  1. Hotels, taverns, etc
  I. Title
  647'.95 TX911.2

  ISBN 0-85038-791-4
  ISBN 0-85038-792-2 Pbk

Phototypeset by Kerrypress Ltd, Luton

Printed in Great Britain by The Anchor Press and bound by William Brendon & Son Ltd, both of Tiptree, Essex

Contents

Introduction

Everyone wants to run a wine bar. Advertising executives, Lloyd's brokers, bank managers and general businessmen all seem to have a hankering for early retirement into the catering trade and wine bars are seen as a gateway to a new life. Every one of these professions and many more are represented among the UK's current 2000-plus wine bar owners. Some are very successful, others go bust quite quickly and in some areas wine bars come and go with startling regularity!

The wine bar is a fairly modern phenomenon. It first appeared in the early seventies and has gained in popularity ever since. Unlike some catering fashions, the wine bar looks all set to stay around for a good many years more, and despite the growth so far there still appears to be plenty of room for expansion. Wine drinking is on the increase and even the pubs are jumping on the bandwagon.

What is a wine bar?

The answer to this question is not as obvious as it may seem. Some so-called wine bars are converted pubs and the pub atmosphere still clings to the woodwork. Others have only a restaurant licence and customers are obliged to eat with their drink.

The essence of a wine bar is that customers can walk through the door without being committed. They can have a single glass of wine or a bottle or two, or they can have a snack or a full meal. The atmosphere is informal and friendly. In the past there were establishments such as Yates Wine Lodges and Henekeys which concentrated on the sale of wine but food was either absent or entirely secondary. Nowadays wine is still the operative word but the trend is for people to eat when they drink out and food has become increasingly important.

The actual pattern of wine and food sales will vary according to the time of day and the location of the wine bar. Lunch-time trade may see the odd drinker or two but it is far more likely to be made up of snacks for office workers and shoppers, and business lunches. Wine bars are often popular with people who wouldn't normally be pub or even cafe users and women form an important part of this group.

In the evening there may be a casual pre-dinner or theatre drinks trade with a later evening meal clientele or, in inner city areas, business may dry up completely once the after-office drinkers have gone home. At the other end of the scale many small-town wine bars do not open their doors in the evening until 7.30 pm or so when they know the dinner trade will be arriving.

All shapes and sizes

Wine bars come in all shapes and sizes; their food and wine lists, their ambience and decor, are as variable as the personalities of their owners.

First, there are large wine bars seating up to 200 people. These tend to be in the big city centres and their success is based on a high-volume trade. The prices are reasonable and the food, though simple in nature, is a main supporting factor. Service is usually at the bar or counter and lunch-time customers are not encouraged to stay for too long.

Some of these wine bars, like Coolings in Exeter and Hawkins in Birmingham, are privately owned. Others are part of wine bar chains or are owned by catering companies and breweries. Very often they are on two floor levels, making attractive use of cellar and basement areas, and they are usually fairly spacious with plenty of standing room around the bar. They require a fair number of staff and a high degree of management ability.

Larger wine bars sometimes deliberately set out to capture young people in the evenings and there may be a disco or live music. Converted pubs often fall into this category. Others are looking for a quieter clientele but, as in some London wine bars, they can still have the advantage of acting as a social centre for a slightly older age group.

At the other end of the scale is the small bistro style of wine bar. These could be located anywhere but actually seem to be particularly popular in small country towns, perhaps because they provide a reasonable alternative to eating at the local Chinese or Indian restaurant. They may seat up to 40 or 50 people and the decor is designed to look more like a restaurant with check table-cloths and little standing room. The overall area is much smaller than in the large wine bar and there will be far fewer staff. However, the owner will be able to charge rather more. Most customers eat a full meal, particularly in the evening, and at the more successful ones booking will be essential.

Somewhere in the middle is the small to medium-sized wine bar which concentrates on the cheaper end of its wine list but which can offer up to 50 or 60 and maybe even 100 different wines for more discerning customers to choose from. The food may be cold and simple or it may be fairly elaborate but the customer is not pressurised into eating.

The decor is informal but comfortable and may range from re-cycled church pews and converted sewing machines to old pub chairs and tables. The fact that it is a wine bar is shown in the lack of table-cloths, bare floors and plenty of chalkboards.

In inner city areas the emphasis may be on businessmen's lunches and the London-based Davy group of wine bars is a very good example of a company which has found a really workable formula. The decor is very much 'old wood and sawdust' and there are plenty of dusty bottles and barrels in evidence. They are all dark, candle-lit

ry inviting. Indeed, the ambience of this
of wine bars is perhaps even more important
than the food and wine which, though of high
quality, tend to be limited in scope. Maybe they are
designed to appeal to the conservative nature of
the city gentleman!

Other wine bars, large and small, are attached to
hotels or restaurants. These have both advantages
and disadvantages but they are really beyond the
scope of this book.

What makes a good wine bar?

This really is a difficult question to resolve but a
large part of the answer must lie in the person who
is running the wine bar. He or she can really put
their stamp on the place by sheer force of
personality. Having said that, then the quality of
the food and wine and the ambience are equally
important. Of course, there are many successful
formulas and if you are thinking of opening your
own, a tour of as many wine bars as you can find
will help you to decide upon the important factors.
Have a look at the *Which? Wine Guide* too, for this
lists over 100 wine bars in London and 100 around
the country which are successful enough to be
talked about. The guide really covers a cross-
section of almost every type of bar.

The judges of the Gilbey Vintners Golden
Corkscrew Award say that in the wine bar section
they are looking for:

Value for money.
Useful and informative descriptions of the wine
   on offer.
Helpful staff who give confidence to the
customer.

The last point highlights the fact that many people
who come into a wine bar nowadays are drinking
wine, if not for the first time, at least with only a
limited experience of it. They do not want to be
patronised by either the owner or his wine list.

Value for money, of course, means quality. A

wine bar may offer a simple range of salads with one or two hot dishes, it may offer steaks and jacket baked potatoes or it may offer a full bistro-style menu. What is on the menu is not really all that important. What does matter is that the food is made from the best available ingredients and is prepared with care and attention to detail.

Similarly, the wine list may include only 20 or so low cost wines or it may range from the lower end of the wine scale up to fine and rare wines. What really matters is the attention that has been paid to ensuring the quality of those wines and to keeping the cost within reasonable bounds.

Informality and variety are also part of the stock-in-trade of a successful wine bar. Customers want to feel comfortable in the place and not harassed in any way. Had they wanted the grandeur of white table-cloths, black-suited waiters and a gourmet menu they would have gone to a restaurant. Variety is of course a means of surprising the customers and keeping their interest. They may have found and liked your wine bar but you have to make an effort to keep them coming back.

So you fancy running a wine bar?

Visiting wine bars and assessing their qualities is a very different matter from running one yourself. Too many people have started off with the idle thought that it all looks rather an easy way of making a living. 'I wouldn't mind starting at 11 am, having a drink or two with the regulars and closing up at 3!' runs the spurious argument. 'Then there's the evening session which may be a bit late, but it's very sociable. And think of all the money I and my friends spend in places like these!' After a couple of bottles of claret the guy has convinced himself. Sometimes it is friends who do the encouraging and this can be even more invidious. Many people have been told by friends that they should open a wine bar — and when the friends stop coming there are no other customers.

The reality is that running a wine bar is exceedingly hard work. Richard Gale, who runs a very successful wine bar in the – at first glance – unlikely town of Llangollen, says that he always asks prospective wine bar owners who come to him for advice one question, 'Do you know what hard work is?' To the answer 'yes' he replies, 'Then double it!'.

The wine bar day certainly does not start at 11 am. It is much more likely to be 8 or even 7 am. There is a good deal of preparation required before the bar opens, not least of which is the shopping and preparation of the food. Then there is the cellar to think about, stock to be moved into place, wines to be re-ordered, the cleaning to be supervised and many more small jobs which recur on a day-to-day basis.

Similarly the afternoon recess will be taken up with clearing up after the lunch-time rush and preparing for the evening onslaught. Then, of course, there are all the records and accounts to be kept up to date. These financial chores really do take up a lot of time and a good 50 to 60 per cent of the wine bar owners I have spoken to were so busy during the day that the accounts were an evening or even late night activity.

If you are not daunted by hard work then you might cast a look at your social life. Do you have lots of friends you like to visit and entertain and does your family like to spend time together, on shared activities, hobbies or outings? Because all of this is likely to go by the board too. As one wine bar owner commented to me, 'Running a wine bar isn't an occupation I'd recommend to anyone who likes a busy social life. Our social life revolves round the wine bar and its customers. We believe that making customers feel at home and part of the party we are enjoying is one of the main reasons why our regulars are regulars.'

Of course, this aspect of the life may be part of the attraction, but does your partner feel the same way? If both of you are fully involved in the business it can work well and of course it helps to split the workload and cut down the numbers you need to employ. But quite a few marriages have foundered on this particular rock. If your partner is not deeply involved in the business, he or she may easily come to resent the time you spend there.

Holidays, too, can be a bit of a problem. But Judith and Michael Rose of Boos Wine Bar off Marylebone Road in London find that, though they completely shut up shop for two periods of two weeks each year, their customers always come back as soon as they return. Judith and Michael have one holiday in the late summer when they go on a wine tour to increase their wine knowledge and contacts, and another in the winter which is their real break.

Another point raised by many wine bar owners concerns the ability, quite simply, to put up with people, because, of course, the wine bar day is not one long party. People can be difficult, stupid and petty as well as friendly, interesting and fun. Remember that you will be dealing with people day in and day out, without much let up. You cannot just decide to stay closed for a day, or if you do you will soon lose custom. So can you smile through thick and thin?

Finally you should ask yourself if you are completely unflappable. The day I visited Richard Gale in Llangollen he had just dealt with a coach load of 40 American tourists, virtually single handed as the day was normally a slack one. Crises are also bound to occur with staff, with non-delivery of essential supplies or with breakdown of vital equipment. So be prepared.

Here is a checklist of points to think about before committing yourself to the wine bar game:

Checklist for a prospective wine bar owner

1. Have you made a realistic appraisal of your aptitude for going it alone? You will no longer be an employee and will probably be an employer.

2. Are you prepared for really hard work?
3. Will your partner support you and if necessary work just as hard?
4. Do you mind relinquishing your social life for one with people who may not be quite so congenial?
5. Can you put up with people day in and day out?
6. Are you reconciled to having virtually no free time at all?
7. Are you completely unflappable?
8. Do you have good health?
9. What are you best/worst at in your present job and how might this relate to running a wine bar?

If you cannot find a positive answer to the great majority of these questions the wine bar business is not for you. And it's no good thinking that you might run a small one on a part-time basis. Gill Sinclair and John Clemmett of Brahms Wine Bar in Bishop's Stortford tried this. Gill was a journalist and therefore a fairly free agent, and John was in local government. It took them a single week to realise that running a wine bar is not a business which can succeed on a hobby basis. They now employ a regular staff of four plus a rota of eight part-time staff and still work a 90-hour week in the wine bar themselves. They count themselves lucky to have an evening off together every two or three weeks.

Generally speaking running a wine bar is a lifestyle in itself but there are exceptions. If you are in partnership with someone who is trustworthy and keen to work in the business then the workload is relieved a little. But in my experience all those wine bar owners who have taken this course have been keen to build up an even bigger business, and as the load has been eased in the first wine bar, so they have gone on to open the next. They just have the wine bar bug!

Getting to know the business

Once you decide that you have the right kind of personality to stay the course, attention must turn to the practical considerations involved. Do you know anything about the wine bar or catering business? Do you know anything about business at all?

If the answer to one or even both of these questions is 'no' there is no need to be too daunted. I have come across quite a number of people running successful wine bars without a scrap of previous knowledge. Admittedly, some of them had learnt the hard way and, it must also be said, that there have been plenty more who have gone bust.

However, lack of knowledge can be remedied, and experience in one field can indeed be transferred to useful purpose in another. One ex-RAF officer's only previous experience had been with the officers' mess but he took three months after he left the service to work in a famous London chain of wine bars before he began to look for premises of his own. He was lucky in that he met the owner at a cocktail party and so was able to plead his cause face to face. The result was three months' unpaid work learning the business. He told me he made notes on absolutely everything, including the height and width of the bar, the selection of glasses used, and the facilities in the ladies' loo.

Wine bar jobs both paid and unpaid are fairly easy to come by. Most bars employ a large number of part-time staff and most owners are surprisingly keen to help would-be competitors, though no doubt they would be happier if your wine bar were likely to be in another part of the country. However, experience as a wine bar employee may not fill you in on the management techniques involved and some kind of management training is very important. There is a particular way of looking at a business venture which distinguishes the professional from the amateur.

A number of courses are run both by private

colleges and by polytechnics and night schools which are specifically intended for people who are thinking of setting up their own business. They are designed to point out the difficulties which you may come up against and to give some pointers on how to deal with them. Check for courses with your local education authority. The Department of Trade and Industry Small Firms Service may have an office in your area and they might be able to point you in the right direction for a suitable course.

Another RAF man I've met would certainly have profited from this kind of course for he had been unable to learn anything about the business in advance, having decided to set up the wine bar prior to his retirement. His wife was equally lacking in any kind of business experience. The result was a very bad choice of location, inadequate controls resulting in theft by an unscrupulous member of staff, and a good deal of hard rethinking on the way the bar was to be run. This particular wine bar is now breaking even but it would have gone to the wall without the owner's other income.

Ex-business people are probably in a better position to start up for they should at least understand the necessity for careful budgeting, cash flow analysis and stock control, but the mechanics of the catering trade are different in some ways from other businesses and some prior experience is a great help.

If you have a close friend or a relative in the business you may be able to learn from him. Robin Hotton of the Grapevine in Crediton freely credits his friend Richard Gale with a large part of his own success. Richard was originally a customer of Robin's and Robin helped to find the finance for Richard's Llangollen venture. Some years later when Robin decided to give up his own job he was able to profit from his friend's experience in opening a wine bar. They now swop notes and indulge in some friendly disagreements about the way things should be done.

Experience of management in the catering trade, of course, puts you in a very strong position, for the chances are that you will also have a reasonable knowledge of food and wine. However, these are slightly easier skills to acquire. On the wine front there are plenty of books on the subject, albeit not many of them concentrating on the cheaper end of the market. There are excellent publications such as *Decanter* and *Which? Wine Magazine* to help you on your way. There are numerous courses and plenty of opportunities for wine tastings with both shippers and merchants. So some concentrated homework, coupled with an investigation into what sells well in other establishments, will be a good start.

On the food side, 'good home cooking' is exactly the type of thing that people are looking for and though there are pitfalls in moving up to larger quantities most competent cooks should be able to manage the recipe side of the business.

Chapter 1
Getting Organised

As soon as you take the decision to start your own wine bar and certainly well before you purchase it, you will need to start talking to your bank manager, solicitor and accountant. But even before this you will need to start thinking about what sort of legal entity your proposed business should be.

Legal structure

You have three options open to you. You can run your prospective wine bar as a sole trader, as a partner in a partnership, or as a director in your own or somebody else's company. These are some of the factors which should be considered before making the decision.

Sole trader
There is virtually nothing to stop you setting up as a sole trader at any time and it is a very simple and easy way to trade. However, if you are going to trade under the name of the wine bar you must disclose your own name and the address at which documents can be served if necessary. Under the provisions of the Companies Act 1981 this information must be on your letter-head and indeed on all business documents. It must also be displayed in the wine bar.

Trading as a sole trader means that you are self-employed and can take all the profits from the business, but you are also personally liable for all its debts. This means that your creditors could seize your car or even force you to sell your own home to cover debts incurred by the wine bar.

You will be liable to income tax under Schedule D and will incur VAT, like any other company, when your turnover exceeds £18,000 a year which of course should be immediately. There can be certain tax advantages here which also apply to partnerships but not to limited companies. The commencement rules, for example, can have the effect of basing tax assessments for the first three years on the profits of just the first year's trading. If you can keep these as low as possible you will feel the benefit three times over. This does not mean that you have to make less money but it does mean that certain purchases, for example, might be brought forward so that the allowances on them can be brought into the first year's accounts. And there are other devices which can also be quite legitimately used.

Partnership

This is where two or more people are trading jointly as self-employed. It is just as easy to set up a partnership as it is to become a sole trader. The advantage of a partnership is that the financial and working load is shared. But there are some grave disadvantages. All the members of a partnership are personally liable for its debts. This could mean that you have to fork out on a debt incurred by one of your partners about which you knew nothing. So partners have to be people who trust each other implicitly.

It is also probable that over a period of time there will be disagreement between the partners, even though guidelines were agreed at the start. It is therefore essential that you have a formal partnership agreement drawn up by a solicitor. This is true even of husband and wife partnerships. Start by getting each of the prospective partners to make a list of areas that they feel might possibly give rise to dispute and then give all the lists to the solicitor to sort out. He should be able to draft a form of words to cover all the points raised and he may also come up with some you haven't thought of. Here is a checklist to consider:

Checklist of common areas of dispute among partners

1. How are the profits to be divided: according to the amount of capital put in or to the work put in? How much money can be drawn by each partner, on what basis and how often, in the way of remuneration?
2. Who is responsible for what aspects of the operation?
3. How are major decisions affecting the business to be taken? By majority vote, by the partner into whose responsibility area it falls, or by agreement of all the partners?
4. What items such as cars, telephone bills etc can be charged to the business?
5. What happens when a partner withdraws or retires? How is his share of the business to be valued? What happens when a partner dies?
6. How can existing partners be got rid of and new ones admitted?

Private limited company

The advantage of a limited company is that, in law, it has a legal entity quite separate from that of its owners or shareholders. Consequently, if a limited company goes bankrupt the shareholders are liable only to the extent of their shareholding. They are not liable as individuals and their private assets cannot be touched unless the company has been trading fraudulently.

A limited company can be formed by two shareholders, one of whom must be a director. It must also have a company secretary. In addition to preparing accounts for the Inland Revenue and VAT, it must also have its accounts audited and it must make annual returns to the Registrar of Companies showing all the shareholders and directors, any changes of ownership that have taken place, a profit and loss account for the year and a balance sheet.

The mechanics of setting up a company are quite easy and may be done through your solicitor or through a company broker. Do make sure, however, that the articles of association are sufficiently wide-reaching to enable you to expand your field of activity if you want to in the future.

If you want to get going in a hurry you can buy a ready made company 'off the shelf' from a company broker. It does not really matter if the name of the company is completely unrelated to the name you have chosen for your wine bar. You can trade under the wine bar name in just the same way as you can as a sole trader. All you have to do is disclose the company name and the premises on all business paper as required in the Companies Act 1981. If you are determined to have the wine bar name in the company name a search will have to be carried out to ensure that the name is not already being used. However, it is usually fairly easy to add extra words to distinguish your company from any existing one.

As a director of a limited company you will not be self-employed but will be employed by the company and pay income tax under Schedule E. Salaries and fees are treated as an expense of the company. They are not a distribution of profits but a charge against them, so it is quite possible for a company to show a trading loss after payment of directors' fees but it need not mean that the directors are not paid. Any profits earned by the company after all expenses have been paid are at present liable to corporation tax at 38 per cent up to £100,000, and 55 per cent up to £500,000.

Funding

Having worked out the mechanics of your new business venture and organised professional help in the way of legal and financial advice, the next step is to make an assessment of the kind of money you are likely to be able to raise against the amount you are going to need. This aspect is looked at in more detail in Chapter 3 but you should try to make some sort of estimate of the figures required if only to see whether you can raise even a small percentage of it yourself. The question, 'How much money will I need?' is rather like asking, 'How long is a piece of string?' It will depend upon whether you are planning to buy or rent a property, whether it is large or small and where it is located. Start by making some enquiries into prices and rents in the kind of area you think you would like to operate. Look at the advertisements in the property columns of the newspapers, the wine and spirit trade magazines, and talk to estate agents and you will begin to get a picture of availability and prices. Remember, too, that money will be needed for outfitting if the property is not a going concern and you will need to have a fair sized sum for working capital.

Now have a look at how much money or capital you can put together off your own bat. Do you or your prospective partners have any spare capital? Is there a chance of a second mortgage on your house? Do you have any other assets such as life assurance against which you could borrow? This is an important point even if you are planning on setting up a limited company, for the bank manager will look at the issued share capital and if he feels it is insufficient to back the loan he has been asked to put up, he is likely to ask the shareholders to guarantee a loan or overdraft with their own personal assets. In fact this is the usual procedure in the case of a new company with no track record.

Another possibility might be to borrow from friends or relatives in return for a small share in the business. However, you should exercise some caution here for if you are not careful you could lose control of your own company. You will need to hold slightly more issued share capital in the company than that which is put in by all the others to retain control.

Once you have assessed your ability to raise personal capital, have another look at the figures required for different types of wine bars. You will now be in a much better position to decide which sort of ball game you might be in. Of course, if you do decide to go ahead, you will have to repeat this exercise in much more detail.

Going ahead

So you have decided to go ahead? Now is the time to sit back, unencumbered by the limitations of finance and premises, and decide just what sort of a wine bar you want to run. This may sound a little too much like pipe-dreaming but it is very important to get clear in your own mind exactly what you will be trying to achieve. Of course, you will have to modify your ideas in the light of reality but the essence will remain.

The philosophy that you work out now will colour all the decisions which you will have to make as the venture takes shape, so define it as clearly as possible. What sort of market are you going to aim for? What sort of customers do you want? Do you want a high-volume trade with simple snack food or is the bistro-style wine bar more for you? Do you like the idea of the busy inner city wine bar or do you prefer the quieter pace of a country town?

Whatever the answers are, write them down in some detail and the picture will begin to emerge. From this you will be able to distil some short but succinct notes on what you are trying to achieve. Keep them handy, they will help to remind you what you are after when you are tramping round the places for sale. They could also form a very useful part of any presentation you may need to put together to raise the finance.

If you get it right it is possible to be extremely successful. The Cafe St Pierre, winner of the 1982 *London Evening Standard* Wine Bar of the Year Award, was only in its first year of operation when it won the award, and the Source Wine Bar had been going for less than six months when it won the Gilbey Vintners 1983 Golden Corkscrew Award.

Chapter 2

Location, Position and Premises

'First find your premises and the money will follow,' advised one highly successful wine bar owner, and indeed this advice is not as glib as it sounds. No one is going to lend you money without a thorough briefing on the business you are planning to run and this must, of course, include the premises. If these premises are in a really good High Street location then the money will be more easily forthcoming than if they are tucked away in a quiet cul-de-sac.

Location, location, location

Which brings us immediately to Conrad Hilton's famous quotation that the three most important factors in the siting of his hotels are 'location, loction, location'. This maxim certainly holds good for wine bars too.

So what constitutes a good location? First of all you must be near your potential customers. This may mean nearness to the head offices of a number of companies, a university or large hospital, a busy shopping area or an open market place. It may also mean nearness to a young middle class residential area or even to a resident bed-sitter population. The majority of your business will come from word-of-mouth recommendation, so there needs to be a concentration of people with similar needs and tastes within easy reach.

Second, there should be plenty of people walking past the door. The flow of people down the High Street, for example, will be much greater than that in a residential suburb. If your premises look attractive enough people may be tempted to drop in on the off-chance and try it out. If you are not sure of the passing traffic for a particular set of premises it can be checked by quite literally standing on the pavement, watching and counting. Do this on potentially quiet days as well as on market days and at the weekend. An owner I interviewed worked out that every 10 yards farther from the market place in his country town would have meant a £100 a week drop in turnover.

A useful rule of thumb method for quick assessment of market potential came from Steve Jones who runs the highly successful Pipe of Port in Southend. His advice is to look for the large multiples such as Marks and Spencer and McDonalds. They know a good location when they see one, he believes, for they have plenty of money to spend on this type of market research. The trick is to know what each multiple is looking for and then see if their requirements match your own. Marks and Spencer, says Steve, spell a certain social mix and their customers are definitely wine bar people. Not surprisingly, there is a very large Marks and Spencer store near the Pipe of Port and there is also a McDonalds down the road. The latter, so Steve says, means quantity.

Remember, too, that towns are nothing like as static as they seem. The 'centre' of a town may be moving, through lack of space perhaps, to an open plan area with more car parking, pedestrian freeways and leisure centres. Your wine bar will have a better chance of success if it is where the people are.

Competition

Some people are chary of starting up a wine bar in an area where there are other catering establishments but it really is better to be where the action is than to be far away from all other leisure activities. Wine bars can easily compete with both pubs and restaurants and indeed, if the population is large enough, with other wine bars. Competition can actually help to fill the wine bar in the early stages — people will come in if only from curiosity — and it will help to keep you on your toes in retaining that clientele.

If you are buying a going concern, a wine bar which is in successful competition could be a better bet than one which, though it appears successful, has no competition. Someone may move into that area after you and steal the ground from under your feet.

Where to buy?

The actual decision on where to buy will be governed not only by such considerations but also by what is available and by the parameters set down in your initial planning. You must have a picture in your mind of the size and type of wine bar you want to run and you must have an idea of the kind of money it will be possible to raise.

You should also remember that the purchase is primarily a business one, and even if you are planning to live in the same premises, the decision to settle on a particular site must be based on sound business reasoning rather than personal liking. Any wine bar must at least be able to support itself and also cover the cost of the borrowings.

If your preference is for a large wine bar with a high turnover you must be sure that there will be enough trade to fill the place, and this probably means a large town or city site. Your choice will be limited simply to which one. London, of course, has been the magnet for wine bars but unless you feel sure that your formula will work in this rather fickle capital you may do better elsewhere. London is pretty crowded with wine bars.

David Belford and his wife wanted to run exactly this type of wine bar. They had originally had a restaurant in the Midlands but David preferred the informality of the wine bar atmosphere. They finally settled on Coolings in Exeter which was a going concern but not over-successful. The wine bar is situated in the centre of the city though not on a main thoroughfare. However, there are other catering establishments in the

27

same street and it is by no means off the beaten track.

Coolings can hold a maximum of 170 to 200 people and it is full most lunch times with both shoppers and business people. In the evenings the numbers are a little more variable but the cellar is divided into three sections which can be separated off for private functions. There is a good pre-theatre and dinner trade and in the late evening, the bar is very popular with students from Exeter University. David has turned this city wine bar into a roaring success.

The bistro type of wine bar, on the other hand, can be situated almost anywhere and you are much more likely to be able, given time, to indulge your own personal preference on the sort of place in which you wish to live. I have visited successful bistro-style wine bars in the London suburbs, in industrial centres and in small market towns. The only requirements seem to be a residential population and a gap in the catering market. Nowadays people rarely go to a restaurant except for a special night out, but they do want to go out to eat. The wine bar offers an excellent alternative to the pub, steak house or Chinese restaurant.

The small to medium-sized wine bar proper with a greater emphasis on the wine list than in the bistro type of place also seems to be able to prosper in a variety of locations. London has its fair share of this sort of wine bar tucked away in the side streets of the West End, in the City and in the residential suburbs such as Hampstead, Ealing and Richmond. Out of London they flourish in locations as divergent as Leamington Spa, Ramsgate, Leeds and Llangollen.

Even pretty small towns, if they are carefully chosen, can support flourishing wine bars. Bishop's Stortford and Halstead in Essex are good examples. Bishop's Stortford is a small boom town with thriving industrial and commercial interests. Ambitious young executives have been attracted by this expansion and there are also plenty of London commuters. All of this is good for the wine bar business. Halstead is a little different. Here the purchase price was low and there was very little in the way of evening entertainment. Though not large, the residential population is still sufficient for the wine bar owner to make a reasonable profit.

However, not every small town is suitable. Allan and Pam Diamond confess that their choice of location has not been a very good one. They run Tempters in Middlewich, Cheshire, and thanks to a lot of hard work, good food and a very cheap but interesting wine list they are now full most evenings. Unless there are special bookings lunch times are a dead loss and they now remain closed. The trouble is that, though the wine bar is on the main street, there really is no business in Middlewich. The population is both small and relatively poor and there are few professional people operating locally. It is a town which has been by-passed both by any kind of industrial development and a ring road. There is thus no ready made market on the doorstep and no passing trade, and for a long time no one knew Tempters was there.

Small can also mean city centre. Boos Wine Bar in Marylebone, London is a really attractive example of a small inner city wine bar. The clientele is mainly business orientated and comes from the large office blocks all round it. The executives from the head offices of a major oil company and a leading retail store are often to be seen entertaining · guests or simply enjoying themselves. The bar, at a pinch, will seat 40. The wine list is extensive and the food simple.

As the bar relies on its business clientele it shuts at 8 pm and this can be an attraction for some owners. Not everyone wants to cook every night or at weekends, though Judith and Michael Rose will tell you that the evenings can still be very busy with accounts, records and the like.

In looking at existing wine bar locations, there does seem to be a bias towards the southern part of the country and both Wales and Scotland have great wastelands without a single wine bar in

29

sight. 'Northerners are not wine drinkers', is the usual explanation. But then, nor were the southerners a few years ago, and these areas could be worth looking at as the wine drinking habit slowly spreads.

In the vanguard of this movement is Richard Gale who opened Gales in Llangollen eight years ago. This is a very successful wine bar which draws on a catchment area of 50 miles or more. Country people do not seem to mind driving quite long distances if they like a place. Wrexham, with its growing industrial complex, is not far away and the town has a thriving tourist trade. Everyone thought that Richard Gale was quite mad to start up in a town with such a small population of its own and he had some difficulty getting the money he needed, but he has certainly proved his critics wrong. Of course, he put a lot of care into his choice and his success has been due to some astute thinking as well as to hard work and an original approach.

If you are thinking of opening up new ground it is quite a good idea to look for parallels. If the formula works in Southend, why not in Southport, in the Cotswolds, why not in the Lake District and in Crediton, Devon, why not in Richmond, Yorkshire?

A going concern or new premises?

The first question to consider here is whether or not you plan to buy a going concern and the decision will probably depend upon how much time and money you have. Only if you are in a job that leaves you enough time to travel around the country looking for premises, or if you have enough money to live on for a while, can you begin to think about starting from scratch. It may take some time to find the right kind of going concern but the chances are that it will take even longer to find premises which will be suitable for conversion.

A change of use for premises will mean planning

permission and this can take longer than you might think. You will have to consult solicitors and surveyors and submit detailed plans, and at the end of all this you may not be successful. I have come across numerous wine bar owners whose first choice of premises fell through because planning permission was withheld. Their final resting place was often a hundred miles away from their starting point. Another stumbling block can be the licence and this, too, can take up considerable time.

Once you have got the building it may need to have structural repairs or alterations and the whole thing will need to be decorated and furnished, both of which consume more time and money. The advantage of buying a going concern is, of course, that you can get going straight away. If you don't like the decor it can always be changed at a later date and the wine list and menu can be altered to accommodate your own ideas. But there are pitfalls. It may not be so easy to 'turn' a wine bar which has become thoroughly run down or which has a bad reputation. If, on the other hand, the wine bar is successful customers may resent the changes you decide to make.

Sometimes a going concern will demand a fee for its goodwill but it is wise to be sceptical of exaggerated claims to a fund of long-standing customers. There is no guarantee that they exist and if they do, that they will continue to come after the change of ownership. However, if you are buying a going concern it will be useful to know exactly how well the business is currently doing and you will want to study the account books for the last three years thoroughly. It is also sensible to assess personally the business that is being done in the bar. If you do not have much experience of catering and are planning to make quite a big investment it might be worth thinking about hiring a specialist company to do an independent assessment for you.

Another question which is worth asking, whether you are buying an existing wine bar or a different type of premises for conversion, is why the existing owner is selling. You may have to dig quite deep to get the real reason. There could, for example, be a change in the local planning regulations pending, a substantial rise in unemployment looming or a different type of resident moving into the area. All these could be very good reasons for not buying in that particular area.

It should go without saying that you ought to consult a surveyor before making any final decision and that the legal process of handing over the business in exchange for cash or a loan should be handled by a solicitor. This might add to the overall expenditure but the cost of not taking professional advice could be very much higher. The intricacies of leases can be formidable. If you are buying a going concern, for example, the lease may not have long to run and you must be sure that you have the right of renewal. Otherwise you could be out on your ear after two or three years.

Quite a number of wine bars I have visited had been taken over as going concerns and the Pipe of Port in Southend is one very thriving example. The wine bar had previously been part of the Davy chain of wine bars which are so successful in London. However, the new owner, Steve Jones told me that this one was really only ticking over and was certainly not making the sort of money it is today. He decided that there was nothing intrinsically wrong with the bar and its location except that it had been too far from the Davy centre of operations. Steve and his partners had their own notions of how a wine bar should look, but in the event they decided to shelve these ideas for their next venture as the customers seemed to like the Davy decor. Nevertheless, they did gradually make changes in both the menu and the wine list, retaining the really popular items but adding new and interesting dishes and a wider range of wines. These changes have paid off so well that Steve is now actively looking for a second wine bar.

Exceedingly attractive and successful wine bars have also been started from scratch. The owners

have been able to put their own ideas into practice
and to plan, within the limitations of the building,
the most efficient pattern of kitchen, bar and
eating area.

The premises

All kinds of buildings have been converted to use
as wine bars and some of the most unusual and
inconvenient have made the most attractive bars.
Stables, garages and outhouses offer one line of
thought, shops and other business premises
another. Even domestic buildings have been converted. There are wine bars under railway arches,
in deconsecrated churches and even on a floating
barge.

However, there are a number of important points
which it is useful to bear in mind when considering
premises for use as a wine bar. The first question
is, does it have a cellar? This is not just for the
storage of wine and other items but is also an
important consideration for the bar itself. Ideally,
wine bars should be in basements or on the ground
floor but no higher. As one wine bar owner put it,
'People like to go downstairs for a drink and then
to climb up the stairs afterwards. They are not
keen to do things the other way round'.

The location of water pipes and mains services is
another important consideration which could
affect your layout of kitchen, service areas and
cloakrooms and even if they do not completely
dictate the location of these areas, they could make
the bar much more expensive to lay out than
originally planned.

If the premises are going to need extensive recon-
struction you should check that the main walls are
strong enough to take the changes and whether
there are any retaining arches and beams which
cannot be moved. Structural conversion work at
Wildes in Leamington Spa, for example, had to be
quickly stopped when a partition wall turned out to
be a structural support and an arch over the bar
started to slip. The bar area ended up a rather

different shape from that planned by the architects.

Access and car parking are other considerations which are sometimes overlooked. Parking on the street can cause a local nuisance which could give rise to complaints. This in turn could affect your licence. Do the premises have a garden or patio which could be used for barbecues and outdoor eating and drinking in the summer?

And last but by no means least there is the question of size. The property may be freehold, leasehold or simply for rent. Whichever it is, the size must be such that the likely turnover will cover the costs of running the place plus rent or interest repayments. A very small wine bar in an expensive property area, for example, may just not generate sufficient income. If, however, there was room for extension into outbuildings which would not cost too much to renovate, the increased size of the resulting bar could make the required turnover.

How and where to look

If you have not already done so, this is the time to write out a specification for yourself. Try to think of all aspects of your proposed bar and make a note of each of them. This will help you to check later how far from your ideal you might have to go, and to choose those areas in which compromise will be the most acceptable. The headings will include some or all of the following:

Type of location: city centre, suburbs, county town etc.
Approximate size: floor space and possible number of covers (people who can be served seated).
Going concern or new premises.
Complete building or part thereof.
Freehold, leasehold, rental.
Approximate cost range.
Cellars and storage areas.
Kitchens.

Living accommodation.
Services and amenities.

Armed with your specification you are now ready to start looking. Premises for sale are advertised in all kinds of publications, though if you are looking for a going concern, a special publication such as *Wine Press,* the *Publican, Catering,* and *Catering Times* may be the most useful. The national newspaper property columns will also be worth looking at.

The main source of information about property on the market is, of course, estate agents but many of these tend to be very locally organised. However, you must begin somewhere so choose the areas at the top of your list and start there. It might also be worth talking to a wine bar specialist in London. Christies and other companies have special property sections dealing specifically with wine bars. Certainly, if you are looking in the London area, these specialists are essential.

You may be lucky but the chances are that you will be looking for some considerable time and may well end up on the other side of the country from that in which you started. Steve Jones wanted a place in the Greater Manchester area and ended up in Southend, and James Walker of Wildes started off in Yorkshire and finished up in Leamington Spa. In each case the search lasted some months and their stories are typical of many others. After spending many hours travelling to and from his home base Steve quite literally took to the road. He hired a motor caravan and looked at dozens of premises in London, Stratford and York among other places before landing on the Pipe of Port.

Once you have found what you believe to be suitable premises, take your time. Do not rush into anything. This is particularly important if the premises happen to be the first you are offered. Check all the attributes against your list of specifications, talk to people who know the locality and, if possible, who also know the catering or wine bar trade. Take the advice of your accountant and solicitor who will, respectively, assess the financial value of the purchase you are hoping to make and the legal commitments involved.

Sit down and look in detail at all aspects of the purchase. Ask yourself the following questions.

1. Are the premises located near the right type of working or residential population for your requirements?
2. Is there a passing trade?
3. Have you checked the trends in the town centre, the other businesses and the competition?
4. Are you totally convinced that the right market is there for your type of wine bar?
5. Is the building really suitable for your purposes?
6. Can you afford the changes or redecoration which may need to be carried out?
7. Have you checked that all the facts you have been given are correct and that planning permission, licences etc really have been granted?
8. Is the price right – the lowest you can get?
9. Do your professional advisers, accountant, surveyor and solicitor, agree that the purchase is a sound one?

In-depth research

Once you are certain that you have found the right property, it will be well worth doing some more market research on the area. The information gained will strengthen your business proposition and could help with the raising of capital. On the other hand, the research could throw up some unexpected information which might just save you from making a bad mistake.

Here are some of the factors to check in more detail:

Local population trends, taking in towns and villages within a reasonable catchment area.

Remember that in the suburbs of a large city, the real catchment area will probably be smaller. Is the population expanding or decreasing? Figures for the past five years should show the trends.

Income trends and age range. What kind of average income is there in the area? Assess this by looking at the kind of property in the area and talk to rate assessment officers and local estate agents. What is the age range of the local population? Is it predominantly young people with children or is it a retirement area?

Business, industry and employment. What is happening to business in the area, is it expanding or decreasing? Is it changing in any way and will these changes affect your business? What are the employment trends? Are there any really large businesses, government departments or large insurance companies in the town?

Tourist trade. What influx of visitors is there each year? How many and what type of people?

Set all this information out in such a way that the salient facts can be seen at a glance and add it to your business proposals.

Chapter 3

Finding the Money

There are many ways of raising money but whichever one you try you will have to provide some of the money yourself. If at all possible, you should not borrow more than the assets will be worth. This means that you will need to have sufficient money of your own to make a percentage contribution to fixed capital cost and to cover working capital. You will have to show that your business proposition is a sound one.

Using your own money

The first step is to work out how much money you can get together from your own resources. You may have redundancy cash, retirement annuity or plain savings in the building society or deposit account. You may also have easily realisable assets such as stocks and shares or jewellery, paintings and antiques.

Second homes, caravans, boats and other capital items are obvious sources of cash but your home can also be used to raise money. If you bought it before the property boom of the seventies, its current value will be much more than your existing mortgage. One answer would be to take out a second mortgage, another to take out a mortgage on a second house and then sell the present one. The latter could be the better course if you are married as one person cannot take out a second mortgage on the marital home without the permission of his or her partner.

Life assurance policies are another source of cash. Most companies will lend quite a high percentage of their surrender value. Whether the yields are a worthwhile sum depends, of course, on the overall value of the policy and the length of time you have had it. It is certainly worth investigating, for the interest rates on these loans are generally less than on bank overdrafts.

Depending on your circumstances these methods may produce sufficient money to start you off or they may be inadequate. However, if you are planning to go into partnership, the combined cash may be enough to enable you to get a loan for the rest. One wine bar partnership, made up of a husband and wife team plus the wife's sister, was able to raise an initial £30,000 with £10,000 from each partner. They then borrowed a further £30,000 from the bank and their business was off the ground.

Private loans

A good many wine bars are financed by private loans, mainly from family but also sometimes from friends or ex-business associates. Very often these loans are at a lower rate of interest than the current bank rate and this has enabled a business to get going where it might otherwise have had some difficulty. Personal cash, plus private loans and a bank overdraft to deal with cash flow problems make a good financial combination. However, private loans can cause a good deal of misunderstanding and heartache. The lender may believe that he is entitled to a say in the management of the business and even to a share in the profits.

The only way to avoid such problems is to explain to the lender that a loan is not the same as a shareholding, and to have a solicitor draw up the terms of the loan. These should include:

The rate of interest.
The period over which the loan is repayable.
The circumstances in which the loan may be withdrawn.
Any other conditions of the loan.

In some instances the loan is conditional on acquiring shares or the option to acquire them. This means that you will be giving away control of part of the company and you are unlikely ever to get it back.

Sometimes private loans are not made directly but take the form of a guarantee to repay an overdraft if the recipient is unable to. This situation is covered by the Business Expansion Scheme which was introduced in the 1981 Budget. Under this scheme there is an income tax incentive for individuals who invest in certain kinds of new trading ventures and wine bars should qualify. All the details of the scheme are set out in a government pamphlet which is available from any Small Firms Centre.

Bank loans

The bank is probably the most likely source of capital and this may take the form of a lump sum towards the initial investment and/or an overdraft facility to help with the demands upon working capital.

Banks make their profits by lending out the money deposited with them, so even in times of economic depression, the bank manager will usually be willing to lend an ear to your proposals. You are, after all, a potential source of income to him.

The problem is more likely to be how much money rather than whether you get any at all. Larger branches tend to be able to lend larger sums than small local branches. On the other hand, the closer your relationship with your own bank manager, the better it will be from the business point of view. If the local branch has invested in you, it will be much more interested in your operation and, provided that nothing is seriously wrong, will not mind helping you over the odd bad patch. If you have local advisers they will probably know what sort of levels of investment your bank manager is likely to consider. The commonest form of help from a bank is an over-draft and this has the advantage over a fixed loan in that interest is only paid on the actual amount by which you are overdrawn. However, an over-draft facility can be withdrawn at any time without notice and it is unwise to use it to finance medium-or long-term requirements.

In addition to evidence that your business pro-position is a viable one (and more of this later), your bank manager will be looking to see if the money will be secure. This means that he will probably ask for security to be in terms of tangible assets such as fixed assets within the business, in this case the building, or in shares or other assets belonging to the owners in their private capacity. This holds equally true for a limited company as for a sole trader or partnership. The bank manager is likely to look at the paid-up share capital, and then ask the directors to guarantee any overdrafts or loans against their personal resources.

If you are unable to persuade your bank manager to lend you the money you need without unacceptable personal guarantees you may be able to take advantage of the Department of Industry Loan Guarantee Scheme. In this scheme the government will guarantee 80 per cent of a medium-term loan of up to £75,000. Borrowers pay a charge for the loan, part of which is an interest payment to the lender and part a guarantee premium to the Department of Industry. Details are set out in a government leaflet obtainable from the Small Firms Service. Some banks operate their own start-up schemes, so ask for details.

Money from government sources

Most of the grants and special loans organised by the various government agencies tend to be aimed at manufacturing industry and are concentrated on the various development areas. However, if you are planning on a small town or rural locality you might be able to get some help from the Council for Small Industries in Rural Areas (or CoSIRA). A

number of other regional bodies such as the Welsh
Development Agency and the Scottish Development Agency might also be worth contacting. Talk
to your local Small Firms Centre (freefone 2444)
and see what they can recommend.

Other sources of finance

These include the merchant banks and financial
institutions like the Industrial and Commercial
Finance Corporation (ICFC). These organisations
may demand a say in the running of the business
or they may not be interested in getting involved in
businesses which are not yet established. Some are
simply not interested in anything that is unlikely
to have a turnover of less than £100,000. However,
some wine bar owners have been able to persuade
financial houses to make them a loan or to invest
in their shares.

A useful guide to finance houses is contained in
Working for Yourself, The Daily Telegraph Guide
to Self-Employment.

It is sometimes possible to raise risk capital from
private individuals by selling shares in your
company. Stockbrokers, solicitors and accountants in small towns may be able to put you in touch
with such local sources of capital.

Putting together a business proposal

A good business proposal will help to speed your
application for money through the assessment
process of any financial organisation and for some
it will be essential. Bank managers will tell you
that a surprising number of would-be business
people have no idea of the likely profit levels for
their business and have made no assessment of
cash flow. They are therefore very well disposed
when they see a carefully worked out document
containing all the relevant information.

Some proposals will, of course, be more elaborate
than others. Richard Gale, for example, told me
that he had all his information on flip-charts and

got his presentation down to a fine art. But he was battling with the problem of finding money for the first wine bar in Wales at a time when wine bars were only to be found in the big cities.

What your proposals must show is that you understand the business you are entering and have a clear idea of how things are likely to go. The bank manager or finance house loans manager will want to know if you have made any assessment of possible demand, what your experience has been and what the competition is. He will also want to see details of starting-up costs and to know whether you have worked out an estimated budget and a cash flow forecast. On what basis are you going to price your food and wine and do you know what levels of seating occupancy you need to make a profit?

The following contents lists for a wine bar business proposal is based on an actual application and is fairly typical of the more successful ones.

Business proposal for a wine bar

From: Name, position and address of the proposed proprietor or senior director making the application.

1. *Introduction*
   Details in brief of the venture and its location.

2. *Personal and company details*
   Details of the structure of your organisation and who owns it, together with your own history or that of the partners or directors with relevant business or catering experience, qualifications and training courses.

3. *The premises*
   Full agents' details, including accommodation, uses past and proposed, tenure, legal costs, inspections, plans and surveyor's report.

4. *Philosophy and market strategy*
   A detailed account of how you see the wine

bar operating, the sort of place it will be and the sort of customers it will have, together with a projection of the sort of custom it might expect.

5. *Market research*

   Details of all the relevant material gathered in the course of your researches in the area, including a breakdown of population, an assessment of the wine bar potential of that population mix, business and economic trends and, where appropriate, a list of major retail and office businesses in the area.

6. *Financial requirements*

   Details of the money you will need for the purchase of freehold or leasehold and for other items such as architect's fees, fitting out, kitchen equipment, general equipment, crockery, glasses and cutlery, music system, wine stocks, legal and other fees, and contingencies.

   This should be followed by a breakdown showing the money already available from private or other sources and that which is still required.

7. *Staffing*

   Details of staffing levels including a break-down of full-time and part-time staff.

8. *Sample wine lists and menus*

   Details of prices and how they are arrived at, together with information on how many tables will need to be filled to break even.

9. *Budget for the first six months or year of operation*

   A month-by-month estimate of income and expenditure, the latter broken down into food costs, liquor costs, rents and rates, wages, advertising and promotion, insurance, administration, maintenance, general expenses, bank or other repayments and interest charges, contingencies and VAT.

Notes should point out that the budget does not take into account expenses incurred before opening as these will be covered by working capital. They should also give some more details on the way in which the income has been assessed, taking into account holiday periods, possible seasonal variations and may go into a breakdown of different sections of the operation such as wine and food.

10. *Cash flow forecast*
    The same income and expenditure information as that contained in the budget, but instead of averaging the sums out over each month, they are given as actual amounts in the months in which they fall. The first month before opening might also be included here as expenses are likely to be incurred but there will be no income.

11. *References*
    Details of financial and personal referees.

You must make sure that you have covered every eventuality in terms of finance. It is sensible to deliberately add a few thousand after 'thinking of everything' as there is sure to be something you have not thought of or which costs more than you have budgeted. On the other hand it is not wise to over-commit yourself financially. If you really cannot afford to carry out your original plans, it is much better to start off in a smaller way and to build up to them than to borrow too much and find that you cannot make ends meet.

Once you have completed your business proposal you should be able to talk about each aspect of the project both fluently and objectively. This is very important, for you must be able to sell yourself and your wine bar project. If you do not have confidence in it, who will?

Chapter 4
The Legal Requirements

Running a business means taking into account a mass of legislation covering topics as diverse as kitchen hygiene, fair trading, income tax and employees' rights. Some of this legislation may affect you even before you buy your wine bar. You will, for example, need to have planning permission from the local authority if you want to change the use of the building you are buying and you will also need to think about applying for a licence.

Most of the areas concerned are quite complicated and you will usually need to take expert advice but it is only sensible to acquaint yourself with the main provisions of the various relevant Acts of Parliament, lists of which are given on pages 58-9 and 149.

Planning permission

If you are buying a going concern you should not need to concern yourself too much with planning permission, but do check that the current owner does indeed have it. I came across one horror story concerning a prospective wine bar owner who thought that he had a real bargain only to find that the previous owner had not bothered to get planning permission for some extensive alterations at the back of the building and the local council were threatening to close the wine bar down. In other instances, the reason for the sale has been expensive alterations demanded by the council.

If you are buying a property which has been used for other purposes you will definitely have to get planning permission from the local authority for

a change of use and this may also be true for
existing wine bar premises which need extensive
alterations.

Planning permission can sometimes be very
difficult indeed to get and quite a few deals fall
through because of the lack of the required
permissions. Applications are quite frequently
turned down and you should be prepared for
substantial costs in the form of application fees
and fees for legal and structural advice. You may
also have wasted a great deal of time.

In view of all these problems your application
must be well planned and properly researched. The
council will want to know exactly what you are
planning to do and how this is likely to affect the
other properties in the neighbourhood. Details of
all structural alterations will need to be included,
together with an assessment of safety factors,
traffic flow and nuisance and/or amenity value.

Application and licence costs

The cost of getting planning permission can vary
from as little as £50 to £400 or £500. Similarly the
cost of the licence, with solicitor's fees etc can vary
between £100 and £500, depending on the area and
the difficulty of getting the licence. Remember too
that every time you want an extension to a licence
you have to pay a fee, currently £12.

The licence

Obtaining a licence can be almost as much of a
headache as getting planning permission. The
1964 Licensing Act is not really geared to wine
bars which are a relatively new phenomenon, and
this in itself can cause problems. However, there
are various types of licence for which you can
apply. You can also apply for a six-day licence if
you want to close on Sunday, and for licences
which do not require you to be open all evening.

Restaurant licence

This is the easiest licence to get. It is a justices' on-licence which is subject to the condition that the sale of intoxicating liquor is confined to persons taking table meals and for consumption as an ancillary to such meals. This may be acceptable if you plan to run a bistro style of operation but it does mean that you do not really have a wine bar. It could prove to be very restrictive, for all customers must have a proper meal, the service must be at the table and cannot be self-service. You will also have to post signs to say that drinks cannot be served without food and this can be extremely off-putting to new or casual customers.

Some owners, on the other hand, feel that this type of licence makes life easier. The successful ones know that most of their customers will book and so they will know almost exactly how many people they will be catering for at each meal. This certainly removes the threat of large fluctuations which assail some wine bars and helps to cut wastage.

Wine, or beer and wine on-licence
These are on-licences restricted to certain types of intoxicating liquors. A wine-only licence means just that, though strengthened cider and perry may be served as they are deemed to be 'British wine' and therefore, like other British wines, come within the scope of a wine licence.

The beer and wine licence widens the choice for customers a little more but in no circumstances may spirits be served. This licence is less restricting for a wine bar because it does allow customers to come in for a drink only and service at the bar is allowed.

Full on-licence
This is the type of licence granted to a public house and it enables the premises to serve any kind of intoxicating liquor with or without food. The justices may grant an unconditional licence or they can add conditions stipulating no dancing or live music, no juke boxes or gaming machines or no increases in normal licensing hours.

49

Most experienced wine bar owners are agreed that a full licence is extremely desirable. As James Walker of Wildes put it, 'You can sell what *you* want and the customer can buy what *he* wants.' So if at all possible you should aim for a full licence.

Do not be put off by those who say that you have no chance of getting one. A number of first-time owners whom I spoke to felt that they had been very badly let down by their advisers in this area. It had been suggested that they should go for the restaurant licence on the basis that the local bench was known to be against granting any more full licences. What the owners had not been told was that it is often very difficult to up-grade a licence once it has been granted. It is far better to go all out for the full licence and possibly have to settle for a wine-only licence than to be stuck with a restaurant licence right at the start.

Going all out for a full licence can be time-consuming and may involve a good deal of work. You will have to provide full details of the premises with structural plans and layout and you must make sure that the premises have been inspected by the local authority, the fire authority and the police. In addition you may have to prove the need for a wine bar. One wine bar owner even raised a petition with a few hundred signatures to do just that.

Very often the local Licensed Victuallers Association will object to another full licence in the area and their argument may take the form of stating that the pubs all serve wine and there is no need for a wine bar. The only way to refute this is to check for yourself. A 'pub crawl' of all the pubs in the area will determine what kind of wine, if any, is sold and whether anything more than table wine is included. Incidentally you can get details of all the licences in the area from the Register of Licences which is kept by the Clerk to the Justices.

Sometimes the restaurants in the area also join in the objections, so you will need to have at your fingertips all the arguments to show that your wine bar is not a pub or a restaurant and that it serves a different need. You should also be prepared to spend some time in the witness box. Periods of an hour or an hour and a half were not unusual among the wine bar licensees to whom I talked.

If you are unsuccessful in your application, don't give up. You may be able to go back with a better prepared case or you could appeal to the Crown Court. The only problem with the latter course is that if you are turned down there, that will be the end of the matter. If you go back to the lower court you still have the appeal in hand.

The licensing situation is worse in London than in other areas and it can be extremely difficult to get a full licence. Things are also complicated by the fact that no new on-licence can be granted in the inner London area and the City of London without the consent of the licensing planning committee for that area. New restaurant licences are the exception to the rule. New towns also have a special statutory committee which has to submit proposals for new licences to the appropriate minister.

However, the number of existing businesses for sale is also greater in London and applying for the transfer of an existing licence is a much simpler business than applying for a new one. Premises with a defunct licence are also easier to re-license. There may also be a possibility of up-grading an existing beer and wine or wine-only on-licence. If the licence has been in force since 3 August 1961 and has been continuously renewed since that time, the licensee may apply for the licence to be varied to include other types of liquor.

Once you have the licence you still cannot rest on your laurels. The licence will come up for renewal annually and if you have a noisy clientele or cause parking problems, there could well be objections to the renewal. Remember, too, that the renewal application is not automatic. It is the responsibility of the licensee to make sure that application for renewal is made at the correct time.

An excellent booklet entitled *An ABC of*

Licensing Law is published by the National Union of Licensed Victuallers.

The premises

Whether you are planning extensive alterations to your wine bar or are simply intending to carry on everything as it is there are a number of statutory regulations which you would do well to check.

Offices, Shops and Railway Premises Act 1963

This Act makes provision for the safety, health and welfare of workers in offices and shops. As an employer you will be required to register your premises with the local authority. Registration form (OSR.1) can be obtained from the local council or Jobcentre. If, however, you do not employ anyone other than immediate relatives your premises may be excluded from the Act.

The general provisions of the Act include requirements on fire precautions, cleanliness, ventilation, lighting, toilets and washing facilities among other things. An abstract of the Act and of regulations made by the Minister of Labour (OSR.TB) should be kept posted in the wine bar for the information of your employees.

The Health and Safety at Work Act 1974 has been superimposed on other legislation. It is wider in scope and takes in all persons at work, including the self-employed (see page 144).

Occupiers Liability Act 1957

This Act covers the general duty of the occupier of premises to all visitors to take reasonable care, and to see that the visitors will be reasonably safe during their visit.

Fire Precautions Act 1971

Premises which provide sleeping accommodation for staff or guests may be affected by this Act, so check up on it if you are planning to augment your income by taking in bed and breakfast customers.

The Food and Drugs Act 1955

This is the 'umbrella' Act for all the regulations relating to the preparation, composition and sale of food. The part of the Act which is immediately relevant is Section 16 which requires you to register with your local authority, usually in the form of the Department of Environmental Health.

The Food Hygiene (General) Regulations 1970 is the legislation under the Food and Drugs Act which will immediately affect you. They set out the general requirements for the cleanliness of the premises, particularly the kitchen areas, the hygienic handling of food and the cleanliness of the people involved in the preparation of the food. The Regulations are enforced by the local authority, some of which issue extremely useful guidelines.

In any event it makes sense to call in the Environmental Health Officer at the outset. It is obviously better to plan your premises with his advice to hand than to go ahead and possibly have to make expensive additions or alterations after the work has been carried out.

The Regulations take in the structural make-up and surfaces of the kitchen, ventilation, work space, lighting, washing facilities, equipment, counter service, storage, drainage, and flooring and ventilation in the dining areas. A careful reading of the Regulations or notes on them can be extremely useful in that it may well throw up areas which you had not taken into account. Music systems, for example, also need sound insulation; potato peeling machines need adequate traps before discharging into the drainage system, and dim lighting needs to have the facility to be turned up to full strength for cleaning and maintenance.

You will need to provide architect's plans, drainage plans and detailed drawings of general layout, ventilation and the provision of sanitary accommodation when registering.

Local authority by-laws

Local authorities vary both in their interpretation

of the various Acts and in their own by-laws, so make sure that at the outset you talk to the District Surveyor and the Fire Officer as well as the Planning Officer and Environmental Health Officer.

Fair trading

This is another heading under which there are a variety of Acts needing to be considered. These include the Sale of Goods Act, the Consumer Credit Act, the Trade Descriptions Acts and the Weights and Measures Acts.

Under the provisions of the Weights and Measures Acts, draught beer and cider may only be sold in quantities of one-third or one-half pint, or in multiples of one-half pint. Whisky, gin, rum and vodka may be sold in quantities of one-fourth, one-fifth or one-sixth of a gill or multiples of those quantities and notice must be prominently displayed indicating in which of these measures you are supplying these drinks.

The position with regard to wine is currently much more flexible. Wine sold in carafes can be sold in one-quarter, one-half or one litre measures or in 10 or 20 fluid ounce measures and the wine bar owner must state which of these he is using. But when it comes to wine by the glass there have been no specific requirements whatsoever. However, at the time of writing, the Brewers' Society are working on a code of practice which it is hoped will be observed by all catering establishments and to help facilitate the code, the Department of Trade have introduced three new legal metric measures namely 125 ml (millilitres), 150 ml and 175 ml.

The code of practice is expected to recommend that wine bars should choose two measures to offer their customers, either metric or imperial, from set lists of measures. These lists run from 100 to 250 ml and 4 to 8 fluid ounces. The two chosen measures should be separated by 2 fluid ounces or 50 ml.

If this practice is generally adopted the customer

will be in a much better position to compare the real prices of glasses of wine and check on which establishments are really offering value for money. This should remove much of the criticism that has been levelled at the wine bar trade. The law already requires you to display the prices of the wine you are serving and the exact quantities will now have to be shown as well.

The prices of food and drink must be displayed in a way which not only allows the customer to see them clearly when he comes to the bar to make his choice but also to see them from the outside when passing by. If you are offering fewer than 30 items of food and drink apart from table wine, all of them must be listed. However, if you have a larger list than this, only 30 of them need to be displayed but they must be representative of the whole.

All prices must be inclusive of any VAT applicable, and if there are any extra charges, such as a service charge, these must be clearly shown. If you run out of something you must remove it from the menu or price list as soon as possible.

The Trade Descriptions Acts are, of course, concerned with the accuracy of your descriptions of food and drink. If, for example, you are claiming to use cream or butter in a dish these ingredients must be used. And it goes without saying that your liquor must not be tampered with in any way. This area is covered by both the Food and Drugs Acts and the Alcoholic Liquor Duties Act 1979.

The Consumer Credit Act 1974 requires businesses which offer any kind of credit to have a licence. However, credit may not be given for liquor consumed on the premises unless it is supplied as part of a meal and is paid for with the meal. The Act does not apply if the transactions are less than £30 in value and your business is not a limited company. However, if your wine bar specialises in business lunches you may want to give credit facilities to your major customers, so remember to check the Act at that stage.

Running the company

Taxes

Once you set up in business you become liable for income tax or company tax depending on how you have decided to organise your business (see pages 19–22). You will also be liable for value added tax. VAT, unlike income tax, is calculated on the amount of money you turn over rather than on the amount you make after paying all expenses. This means that you will be liable from the start. The base limit is currently £18,000 and though this may be raised you would not be very successful if your turnover was anywhere near this level! The VAT inspectors are usually extremely helpful and will certainly pay you a visit to make sure that you understand exactly what is required of you. Your local VAT office will be listed under Customs and Excise in the telephone directory.

If you were an employee and are now self-employed, you will need to notify the local Department of Health and Social Security of your change in status. If you are employing staff, you will also need to talk to the DHSS about National Insurance contributions under the various Social Security Acts. The provisions of these Acts are fairly complicated but leaflets issued by the DHSS do help employers to understand the duties and obligations laid upon them. Employing staff will also involve you in Pay As You Earn tax deductions (PAYE), and you will be bound by the provisions of the Employment Acts and the Health and Safety at Work Act 1974. See Chapter 10 for more details on employing staff.

Insurance

This is an essential part of the planning of your business. Indeed some forms of insurance, such as your liability as an employer under the Employers' Liability (Compulsory Insurance) Act 1969, are a legal necessity. This particular Act requires employers to take out approved policies of insurance with authorised insurers against liability for bodily injury or disease sustained by their employees in the course of their employment. This Act applies even if all your staff are part time.

Your customers, too, need to be protected and you should take out some form of public liability insurance in case you inadvertently cause food poisoning or some other kind of injury to your customers. You will also need third party public liability if you employ staff or work with partners.

The business itself also needs to be protected, so take out insurance on the premises, the contents of the premises and the stock. You can also take out a legal insurance policy to cover you against prosecution under Acts of Parliament such as the Employment Acts and those relating to fair trading. Some insurance companies offer 'packaged' insurance deals which, in one policy, cover a number of different types of insurance at lower cost than individual policies.

Insurance companies vary quite considerably in the premiums they charge for different kinds of insurance and it can be a bit of a jungle. The best way to find your way through it is to go to a reputable broker, preferably a member of the British Insurance Brokers' Association. Brokers will tell you which insurances are necessary and which are desirable. They should give impartial advice on which companies are best for which type of insurance and their services are free of charge to the client. You can also sue them if their advice is bad and you lose money, which you cannot do to insurance agents. Nevertheless, you should still get two or three quotes.

It is wise, too, to consult your accountant and solicitor on the choice. There is no point, for example, in choosing one policy which might have more expensive premiums on the basis that the tax advantages are better, if you are not eligible to take up these advantages.Your solicitor will also impress upon you the need to take great care with any areas which might invalidate the insurance. Reasonable care and maintenance of equipment and the like, for example, if neglected could lead to a claim being disallowed.

Your professional advisers should be called in to give advice but the decision is still yours and you cannot leave it all to them. Read all the policies carefully and be sure that you understand exactly what is entailed. Renewal dates should be noted – your broker may forget to remind you and you should check regularly on current replacement values in case the value of any of your policies needs to be increased.

Insurance can be expensive and you may feel that you will be shelling out thousands of pounds over the years, but remember that it only takes one fire or one legal action against you to wipe out years of work. Far better to be safe than sorry!

Checklist of relevant legislation

Accidents and Dangerous Occurrences Regulations 1980
Alcoholic Liquor Duties Act 1979
Articles and Substances in Contact with Food Regulations 1979
Consumer Credit Act 1974
Customs and Excise Act 1952
Fire Precautions Act 1946
Fire Precautions (Loans) Act 1973
Food and Drugs Act 1955
Food and Drugs (Control of Food Premises) Act 1976
Food Hygiene (General) Regulations 1970
Food Labelling Regulations 1980
Food Regulations 1978
Innkeepers Act 1878
Licensing Act 1964
Licensing (Amendment) Act 1980
Misrepresentation Act 1967
Occupiers Liability Act 1959
Price Marking (Food and Drink on Premises) Order 1979
Proscribed Dangerous Machines Order 1964
Public Health Act 1976

Sale of Goods Act 1979
Trade Descriptions Acts 1968 and 1972
Weights and Measures Acts 1963 and 1976

Chapter 5
Setting up the Business Systems

Every business, however small, must keep accounts. This is a legal requirement for both limited companies and for any business which has registered for VAT. As well as HM Customs and Excise who manage the VAT system, you will also have to satisfy the demands of the Inland Revenue. Other records and systems can be extremely useful in telling you whether you are charging the right amount for your food and wine, if you have enough money coming in to cover a particular month's outgoings, which areas of the business are profitable and which need looking at more closely.

All too often wine bar failures have been caused by inadequate record keeping. The wine bar owner often feels that time spent with his customers is much more important than writing up the ledgers. This leads to a mass of paperwork which can take hours to untangle or which may not adequately reflect what has happened.

The more regularly the records are kept the less time it will take to do them and the more accurate they will be. You will also see trends in the business much more quickly and will be able to spot dishonest dealings on the part of the staff almost immediately. This is a very important point for any business but is particularly crucial when you are just starting up and money is tight.

One of the wine bars I visited in the north of England told me of a barmaid who had milked the new business of over £800. The owner had no stock control system in operation and did not always cash up himself at the end of the day. It took him some time to realise that something was wrong and quite a bit longer to work out exactly what was happening.

Using professional advisers

Not everyone has the business experience to set up their own accounts and records and even those who do will still need professional advice in certain areas. It is therefore vital to ensure that you have the best possible help before you start. Go and see local solicitors and accountants well before you buy any premises. Take your time with the choice and find out as much as you possibly can about the different firms before contacting any of them. It is natural to believe that any professional person will do a good job for you but unfortunately this is not always the case.

You will certainly want to employ firms which are located near your own business but do not simply go for the nearest. Your bank manager or friends in the same line of business as yourself may be able to help but if you are new to an area you will have more difficulty.

Avoid the largest practices in town: you will probably be small fry to them and you may get the least experienced of the partners. The fees will be higher too, as the firm will have overheads, such as expensive offices, to cover. A one-man band, on the other hand, may not always be available when you want him. Talk to all the business-orientated people you know in the area into which you are planning to move and make a short list of possible firms. Go and see them all before making your choice.

A good local solicitor will be invaluable; he will know how the bench is likely to react to a licence application and he will probably know what sort of attitude the local council has to planning applications. If he is truly in touch with the area he may be able to save you both money and heartache. Sit down and make a list of all the points on which you will need legal advice and take it with you.

It is not quite so important to have a local

accountant as it is to have a local solicitor but it will probably be more convenient. However, you do need to be sure that one member of the firm will be able to give you personal and reasonably prompt attention whenever you need it.

Your accountant will certainly be able to advise you on the best form of book-keeping for your wine bar but, unless you are prepared to spend quite a lot of unnecessary money, you will have to keep those books yourself. Many wine bar owners prefer to leave the preparation of the final accounts to their professional advisers but it is important to understand the principles on which they are based, for they will provide valuable information about the business.

Accounting records

Book-keeping need not be complicated. In fact, the simpler the records the easier it will be not to get in a muddle. On the other hand there must be sufficient information to cover the needs of the tax and VAT men and your own business assessment.

The essential books are cash books, purchase records and wages books. Unless you are offering credit terms to local businesses or offering credit card facilities, both of which can cost you money, you will not need a sales book or sales ledger.

Cash books
The cash books make up a complete record of all the money coming into the business and all the money going out. The income side of your cash book will record all the money that is paid into your till. This side of the book could be broken down into food, drink and tobacco and into payments by cheque and in cash. The VAT due on each transaction must also be recorded.

The example shown includes a bank column in which are listed payments into the bank from your paying-in book. These are reconciled against the receipts listed daily and the till rolls.

Income side of the cash books

Date	Total £	Food £	Drink £	Off-Sales £	Tobacco £	Other £	am £	pm £	Cash £	Cheque £	Total less VAT £	VAT £	Bank £
1 Oct	585.00	354.25	210.75	-	15.15	4.85	305.00	280.00	548.50	36.50	497.25	87.75	-
2 Oct	592.00	346.00	236.00	-	10.00	-	381.50	210.50	540.50	51.50	503.21	88.79	1,177.00
3 Oct	641.50	321.00	260.50	57.50	-	2.50	331.00	310.50	527.00	114.50	545.28	96.22	641.50

These records will help you to assess the viability of each section of your business and you will soon be able to see whether it is worth staying open in the evening, selling tobacco products or accepting cheques. Total the columns weekly or monthly for an on-going assessment of trends.

These accounts also show you how much VAT you have collected for the Customs and Excise. It is not a bad idea to place these sums in a separate deposit account. In this way you will have the money when it is due and you will have gained some interest on it. If you leave it in the general account it could get spent on general purposes. On the other hand your cash flow may be such that the VAT money will help to tide you over difficult periods. Only a close study of your cash flow forecast will tell you which is the better course for your business.

The other side of the cash book is concerned with recording all your cheque payments out of the business account. Think carefully about all the expenses you are likely to incur and arrange them in categories. Here again the weekly or monthly total will show where your money is going and whether there are any areas which need looking at in more detail. It will also enable you to keep your VAT records up to date.

The category headings on the debit side of the cash books should include the following and, depending on the nature of your wine bar, there may be others you will want to include.

Checklist of cash book debit headings

Food
Liquor – possibly broken down into wine, spirits, soft drinks etc
Rent and rates
Wages – see also separate books
Services – possibly broken down into telephone, gas, electricity, water rates etc
Insurance
Administration

Maintenance
Replacement crockery etc
Miscellaneous
Depreciation
Professional advice
Petty cash – accounted for with separate petty
    cash book
Bank repayments and interest

There should also be three columns at the end to record the total amount spent, the total less VAT and the VAT itself.

List the outgoings in date order and work out a numbering system to reconcile cheque stubs, vouchers and receipts. Enter this number in the cash book and write it on the cheque and the invoice or receipt.

Use a separate book to record petty cash trans-actions such as the purchase of stamps, local travelling expenses and fresh food purchases. Do not forget to include the VAT column and keep as many receipts as possible.

It is in order to cash a customer's cheque with current cheque card back-up but don't let it get out of hand. You are not a banker but a wine bar owner and there may be extra bank charges to pay for a lot of cheques.

If you are unlucky enough to get bouncing cheques, you could invoke the County Court procedures for bad debt. This can be done by a lay person without the need to pay a solicitor but you do need to know the person's address to serve the summons: no good if they have not put their address on the back or have given a false one! Cheque cards do help to avoid this, but make sure that customers are not signing a cheque for more than the guaranteed amount on the card.

Purchase records

Not all your purchases are made in cash, nor are they all paid for immediately. Very often it is in a business's interest to delay payment as long as possible under the terms of the contract or to pay

Purchase Day Book

Date	Purchase Order No	Supplier	Cost without VAT £	VAT £	Cost plus VAT £	Discount details	Date paid
16.10.84	1	Jones wine merchant	1,400.00	210.00	1,610.00	Pay within 28 days	30.10.84
17.10.84	2	Mineral water manufacturer	150.00	22.50	172.50	2½% discount within 1 week	17.10.84
17.10.84	3	Smith the butcher	50.00	–	50.00	–	22.10.84
22.10.84	4	Peters wine merchant	500.00	75.00	575.00	Pay within 28 days	12.11.84
22.10.84	5	Smith the butcher	40.00	–	40.00	–	22.10.84

when it best suits your cash flow. However, if you do not pay out immediately there is a danger of the invoice being forgotten. A purchase day book and possibly a ledger will ensure that this does not happen.

The purchase day book would show the date of each purchase, the supplier, the invoice amount, VAT if applicable, a reference to the purchase order if used, discounts available for prompt payment, and the date of the eventual settlement which will, of course, remain blank until the payment is made.

A purchase ledger records the state of play with each individual supplier and is only really worth keeping if you buy regularly on credit from particular suppliers.

You may also need to keep a capital ledger for expensive items such as your kitchen equipment and for your fixtures and fittings. The method of accounting for these items is somewhat different from that for day-to-day purchases. Capital items depreciate over time and this must be reflected in your balance sheet and profit and loss account. It also affects your tax liability. The best way of writing down capital goods should be discussed with your accountant.

Wages books

If you employ any staff you will need to keep a wages book. This shows gross earnings for each employee together with deductions for tax, National Insurance, pension contributions, also net pay and the employer's National Insurance contributions.

It is much easier to keep all these records if you have the right kind of books and these can usually be bought from stationers and specialist office suppliers. Take some care with your first choice and be sure that the books suit your requirements. Choose those with as many columns as possible.

Record keeping can take some time as each transaction may need to be entered two or three times. A payment for a supply of wine, for example, will involve writing out a cheque, entering the transaction in the cash book, the purchase day book and perhaps the purchase ledger. However, there are business systems available such as Kalamazoo and Twinlock which work on a loose-leaf page with self-carbon backing. This means that all the entries can be made with one set of writing.

Finding the best system for your business will involve talking to the various representatives. Kalamazoo offer a very simple start-up package at around £90 and their wages system certainly makes life a lot easier. If things get really complicated you may want to consider a small home computer. From the records described above your accountant will be able to gather the information needed to compile a trading and profit and loss account, which will show you the net profit made over a set period of time.

Balance sheet
The balance sheet is not an account but a statement of the balances of assets and liabilities remaining in the books after completion of the profit and loss account. It does not show what has happened to the company over a period of time but rather it shows the financial position of the company at a given date.

You do not need to make up a trading and profit and loss account or a balance sheet if you are operating as a sole trader or as a partnership but they are legally necessary if you are running a limited company. They are, however, very useful in giving you information about your business. You may want to know, for example, what relationship your profit bears to the capital employed in the business. You can work this out by subtracting total liabilities from total assets. If you are making a 15 per cent return or more you are doing quite well. The calculation is made by dividing the profit figure by the amount of capital employed in the business and multiplying the result by 100. Remember that the amount you are paying yourself will substantially affect this figure.

A study of the balance sheet will also tell you whether or not you are maintaining sufficient working capital to meet your requirement for new stock or replacement fittings or to pay the wages. Check the current assets against the current liabilities. If they are roughly the same then you could be in trouble if you had to fork out for unexpected repairs or had a period of bad business. Remember, too, that some of those assets are tied up in stock and are not immediately realisable.

Profitability and cash control

It is vital for any business to have a sufficient flow of cash to meet the demands of wages and bills for goods and services. The importance of liquid cash in running a business has been emphasised by the exaggeration of the problem caused by the inflationary period through which the UK has just passed. Too often profitability is confused with liquidity. However, it is perfectly possible for a business to be trading profitably over a period of six months yet be quite unable to pay a bill which is due on a certain date during that period.

It is therefore very important to keep an eye not only on your pricing policy to ensure that your margins are maintained, but also on your cash position. Failure to look ahead can lead to trouble with your essential suppliers and with your bank manager. To estimate what your profitability and your cash needs are likely to be, you should set up and revise at three- or six-monthly intervals a budget and a cash flow forecast. Revise both of these by comparing with the actual performance. In the first instance there will be an element of guesswork so make sure that you are not over-estimating your likely level of business.

Your budget will show the estimated monthly incomings and against these are set the estimated outgoings. Those which are fixed are averaged out over the period, variable costs are estimated for

Sample Budget

	October £	November £	December £	January £	February £	March £
INCOME						
Food	7,860	6,540	11,640	6,210	6,850	7,860
Liquor	7,200	5,850	10,350	4,437	6,537	7,200
Total	15,060	12,390	21,990	10,647	13,387	15,060
EXPENDITURE						
Food	2,620	2,180	3,880	2,070	2,283	2,620
Liquor	2,880	2,340	4,140	1,777	2,615	2,880
Total	5,500	4,520	8,020	3,847	4,898	5,500
GROSS PROFIT	9,560	7,870	13,970	6,800	8,489	9,560
Wages	2,000	2,000	2,750	2,000	2,000	2,000
GWEP (gas, water, electricity, phone)	170	170	170	170	170	170
Cleaning and maintenance	325	325	400	325	325	325
Administration and general expenses	235	235	235	235	235	235
Catering supplies	400	400	400	400	400	400
Travel and other contingencies	550	550	600	550	550	550
Music, advertising and PR	60	60	60	160	160	60
Rates	130	130	130	130	130	130
Insurance	200	200	200	200	200	200
Bank repayments/interest	500	500	500	500	500	500
VAT	2,259	1,858	3,298	1,597	2,008	2,259
Total	6,829	6,428	8,743	6,267	6,678	6,829
NET PROFIT/LOSS	2,731	1,442	5,227	533	1,811	2,731

each month. Do not forget to add in VAT as a cost. At the bottom of the page is the net profit or loss figure and the sum total of these will give you an idea of the overall profitability for the six months in question. Remember that the stock situation may affect your final profitability.

The cash flow forecast shows the same income figures and the same cost categories but in this instance the cost figures are set down only in the month in which they have to be paid. Thus the rent and rates and services appear only every quarter. This is also true of VAT.

This forecast shows a very healthy cash flow but it also shows the sort of fluctuations which can occur from month to month. In this instance the company has been just about trading profitably for the first two months and the very successful Christmas month has enabled it to cover the January VAT payment. However, an unexpected bill in October or November could have meant that the company would have gone into the red and even in March it would be unwise to spend too much on new equipment, for the next VAT payment will be due and there could be other hidden contingencies.

This sort of forecast can show you when difficult situations are likely to arise so that you can go and see your bank manager with the figures and make arrangements for an overdraft facility.

Security

Unfortunately people are sometimes not as honest as they look and in a cash business such as a wine bar the opportunities for 'fiddling' are many and varied. Of course, if the wine bar is small and you are in constant attendance you may be able to deal with all the cash yourself, but in practice you will probably be employing at least one or two people, if only on a part-time basis.

The first step is to install a cash register and to set up stock control systems which can be checked against the bar receipts.

Sample Cash Flow Forecast

	October £	November £	December £	January £	February £	March £
INCOME						
Food	7,860	6,540	11,640	6,210	6,850	7,860
Liquor	7,200	5,850	10,350	4,437	6,537	7,200
Total	15,060	12,390	21,990	10,647	13,387	15,060
EXPENDITURE						
Food	2,620	2,180	3,880	2,070	2,283	2,620
Liquor	5,000	5,000	2,000	2,000	1,000	2,000
Total	7,620	7,180	5,880	4,070	3,283	4,620
GROSS PROFIT	7,440	5,210	16,110	6,577	10,104	10,440
Wages	2,000	2,000	2,750	2,000	2,000	2,000
GWEP (gas, water, electricity, phone)	–	–	510	–	–	510
Cleaning and maintenance	350	250	250	750	150	270
Administration and general expenses	235	235	335	235	135	235
Catering supplies	100	200	1,000	500	300	300
Travel and other contingencies	550	500	750	500	500	550
Music, Advertising and PR	–	–	210	–	500	550
Rates	–	–	390	–	100	100
Insurance	2,400	–	–	–	–	390
Bank repayment/interest	500	500	500	500	500	500
VAT	–	–	–	6,200*	–	–
Total	6,135	3,685	6,695	10,685	3,685	4,855
Balance brought forward	–	1,315	2,840	12,255	8,147	14,566
BALANCE	1,315	2,840	12,255	8,147	14,566	20,151

* adjusted for incoming VAT

The choice of cash registers is vast. The use of the microchip has made cash registers extremely flexible and they can store and process a good deal of information. Some of today's machines can itemise individual sales, work out VAT, record the sales of individual assistants, show percentages and give breakdowns on food, wine and tobacco totals. This kind of breakdown not only helps you to see how your business is going, it can also point to totals which look suspiciously low. Investigation might lead to the exposure of staff pilfering.

Some machines have in-built security devices such as drawers which must be closed before any amount can be rung up. Electronic machines can also have an audit blocking facility which means that the machine will not work without a tally roll so that items cannot be rung up without being recorded.

The use of electronics instead of moving mechanical parts also means that the machines are less likely to break down but it also means that they could be quite quickly superseded by more sophisticated models.

Take some care with your choice of machine and see what the different manufacturers have to say. There is no point in paying for a highly complex machine which will do much more than your business needs. Nor does it make sense to buy one which does not do enough. Rather surprisingly, more than 60 per cent of licensed premises still use the good old-fashioned press-down mechanical cash register with the little flaps which pop up to register the accounts.

Having decided on the type of machine you want to use, the next decision is whether to buy or to rent. Certainly in times of high inflation renting is an attractive proposition, for it conserves capital and eliminates the need for possibly expensive maintenance charges. Renting also gives you the opportunity to evaluate precisely which type of machine is best in practice and you will be able to change to more intricate machines as your business grows.

However sophisticated your cash register and however detailed your stock control systems (see pages 118–20) you will still need to keep your eyes open for staff fraud, and if you think this is just the product of a nasty suspicious mind, talk to wine bar owners and see how many of them agree that losses due to dishonesty can be a major problem.

There are a number of different types of fiddle, some very simple and others which are quite complicated. Indeed, one wine bar manager went so far as to buy his own till, which he kept hidden in the basement. On the evening he was on duty he came in early and replaced one of the company tills with his own and naturally he made sure that all the money he took during the evening went through that till!

Transactional fiddles are very common. These include under-ringing the total amount on the cash register, not ringing at all or taking money for two transactions and only ringing one of them on the till. The customers might notice these frauds but usually they are too busy chatting to their friends to notice what is going on with the cash register.

Under-ringing is by far the commonest fraud and members of staff get away with it partly because they are often left to cash up themselves. This makes it very easy for them to extract the extra cash at the end of the day. If you yourself take the money out first, count it and then ring up the totals, you will make it more difficult. However, clever staff can still extract the money they have under-rung before you cash up and a detailed tally roll such as those on modern tills can point to what is going on.

Something to watch out for with electronic tills is that the prices may be rung up for the customer to see, but if the appropriate keying-in key is not pressed then nothing will be registered on the tally roll.

Another fiddle I came across had been a real problem in a wine bar in the Midlands. Customers were all served at the table and their bill slip was presented immediately and often paid immediately. In those instances where the customers called for a second bottle or second round of the same drinks, they were re-presented with the same bill and the waitress pocketed the second payment. The same bill might also be presented to another set of customers who had made this same choice of food and drink. Sometimes the waiter or waitress simply says, 'That will be £x,' and does not present a bill at all.

Collusion between staff and customers can also lead to loss and in one bar where students were employed on a part-time basis the 'freebies' to fellow students mounted up to 5 per cent of all the losses in the bar.

Topping-up is another practice to look out for. The house wine is particularly vulnerable to this fiddle. The member of staff simply collects all the wine which has been left in the bottles and uses it to fill a new bottle of 'house' wine. There is no stock loss with this practice but there will be a loss in sales and if the practice is heavy it could show in a drop in the figures. Even more serious is the possible loss of goodwill from the unlucky customers who get the topped-up bottles.

Straight pilfering of goods is another problem area. Half an expensive gateau may go missing and if you do not have good control systems from the kitchen it may go unnoticed. Items like this can add up after a while. The only way to spot this type of pilfering is to check whether the average take-up of each dish each day or week falls off. If you do have reason to suspect this is due to pilfering, tighter controls are the only answer. If you personally count 12 plates of smoked salmon, say, into the bar, you will want to be able to account for these on the tally rolls or bills.

Sometimes you may suspect fraud or pilfering but not be sure of quite where it is happening. In this case ask some friends to come in and observe everything that happens at the table and at the till. They may see something which is obviously stopped when you yourself are present.

Office and business procedures

If at all possible find a corner in the wine bar or in your own home to use as an office. It is extremely important to have a place to keep all your records, correspondence and account books, where you can work undisturbed.

Think about producing special stationery for the wine bar. Buy in bulk but don't overdo it or you will simply add to your storage problems. One Yorkshire wine bar owner had been cajoled into having 500 wine lists printed on the basis that they would be cheaper per item than 100. They were taking up valuable space and had started to go brown at the edges. They were also virtually useless as so many changes had taken place in the list since it was first printed.

Bulk purchasing on certain items of food will make more sense and it is certainly worth joining one of the local cash and carry outlets. However, check them out first as they vary in the discounts they offer and some are not much cheaper than local shops, yet cannot always offer the same quality. If you buy regularly from local suppliers you may be able to negotiate special terms. Check on the markets, too, for these are almost always cheaper than the High Street shops, but watch the quality.

Chapter 6

Name, Decor and Atmosphere

Choosing a name

Your wine bar will, of course, need to have a name and the choice needs careful thought for it can set the tone for the whole operation. You should by now be clear in your own mind about what type of wine bar you want to run, so choose a name which will be in keeping.

Ideally the name should be a memorable one and this usually means something short and to the point. Choose names which are easy to pronounce and thus easy to communicate. However, there are exceptions and long names or slightly esoteric ones, if they are appropriate to the atmosphere of the place, can work. But if you have a look at the wine bars listed in the *Good Wine Guide* you will see that most of them are pretty short.

Names fall mainly into four categories. Examples of each are given below. Have a look at them and see which type you think will be most appropriate for you. Then if you go for a name based on location or on a personality you can start doing some research.

The proprietor's name

Very often the proprietors choose to use their own names and, as the atmosphere in a wine bar often depends largely on the personality of the owner, this is a good idea and nothing like as conceited as it may sound. You may prefer your surname – as in Gales of Llangollen – or you may opt for your Christian name or names, such as Colin's, Max's or Angela and Peter's. In London Bill Bentley opted for his full name.

The location

Wine bar owners have often used their locations as the source of their inspiration. Examples are Downes in Downe Street and Hollands in Holland Park Road, both in London. The Old Bank House in Lymington presumably refers to the previous use of the site and the Archduke on London's South Bank makes oblique reference to the concert halls in the vicinity. There may be a famous landmark nearby or you may be as enterprising as the proprietor of the Wine Barge who has probably the only wine bar afloat.

The booze

By far the most popular names are those which have a connection with wine or with drinking generally. Bubbles, the Wine Vaults, the Wine Press, the Grapevine, the Cork and Bottle, Decanter, Bacchus, Le Beaujolais and Shampers are just a few of them. A little different but in the same general area is Brahms and Liszt with its reference to drinking via cockney rhyming slang!

Themes

Other names have been chosen with reference to local or national characters or to specific events and they are used as the decorative theme for the interior of the wine bar. Examples are Wildes in Leamington Spa and Winkles in Bayswater. Sometimes the link is tenuous indeed. Wheels in Barnstaple, for example, takes its name from the wagon wheels which are used as part of the rustic decor.

The next step is to decide whether you are going to qualify the name by adding the words 'wine bar' or 'food and wine bar'. This decision will probably depend upon which part of the country you are in. London wine bars are part of the normal choice of eating and drinking establishments and one look at the bill of fare will tell potential customers what it is. The words 'wine bar' in small print are usually quite sufficient.

However, experience in other areas has shown

that many people are not quite sure what the words 'wine bar' entail and the addition of the word 'food' has made it clear that meals are being served as well. In the north of England wine bars are often equated with wine lodges which nowadays are not quite the same thing!

Do remember to check that the name you have chosen is not being used elsewhere in the area. You do not want your hard work to build up someone else's reputation. Look in the Yellow Pages for the names of other establishments around you. Remember, too, the provisions of the Companies Acts and the licensing laws and post your name or company name and legal business address in appropriate places.

If you are buying an existing wine bar you may decide to leave the name as it is, but before you start trading, check out the bar's previous reputation in the area. You may decide that a new name is a good idea.

The decor

The premises are now yours to do with as you will or as you can afford and once again it is straight back to your concept of what the wine bar will be. If, however, you have bought a going concern you will need to decide whether it would be better to leave it as it is. This was Steve Jones's decision at the Pipe of Port in Southend. The bar had been part of the Davy group of wine bars and Steve felt that the very attractive decor was popular with existing customers.

Very often the decision goes the other way, perhaps because the place is in need of re-decoration or it is just not very attractive. And of course, premises which have not been used for a wine bar before will need a complete redesign and refit.

The first step is to brief the experts as fully as possible. Whether you are working with an architect, an interior designer and a food services consultant, or simply with a builder and a painter and decorator, they need to know exactly what you are trying to achieve.

To clarify matters in your own mind go back to your original notes (see page 24) and to your market research of the area (see page 36) and re-define exactly who your potential customers are likely to be, what are their likes and dislikes and what are they likely to want? The answers here become the basis for all other decisions.

On your potential customers' desires depend the structure of the wine list and menu, the way they are to be served and last, but not necessarily least, the environment in which they are going to feel most relaxed. Eating and drinking out are social occasions and the atmosphere, when the place is full, should be convivial.

Talk all this through with the experts and see what they have to say about any limitations imposed by the size, shape and design of the building itself.

The practical approach

You will also have some fairly fixed ideas by this time about the feel of the place. You may be mad about nostalgia or Victorian England or perhaps you may incline towards the wine cellar look with vaulted ceilings and bare walls. Whichever concept you have in mind the business consider-ations must come first. Here are some of the factors which must be taken into account in any design.

Customer capacity

How much of the total area is or can be designated for customer use? Remember that this is the money earning part of the wine bar and there will be a minimum number of customers you must be able to serve to make the place pay (see page 34). Obviously if you can get in more than this without increasing the other overheads, such as wages, too much, you will be potentially even more profitable. Work on a basis of 15 square feet per person, which will allow for gangways, chairs and tables.

However, you cannot cram customers in like sardines and though wine bars are far less formal than restaurants, customers will usually want to sit down to eat and not be too jostled on either side. Some wine bar owners pack their premises full of tables and chairs and there is little standing room at the bar. This is fine if you are aiming at a bistro-style operation or if you have only a restaurant licence, but a real wine bar should have an area where customers can stand and have a glass of wine with perhaps an easy-to-eat snack. Research has shown that people prefer a long bar to a semi-circle or square.

The successful Bubbles, Cork and Bottle, and Shampers chain of London wine bars all have a bar area with high stools and plenty of standing room and these areas are always packed at lunch time and are surprisingly full in the evenings too. So if you are aiming to attract 'drinking' as well as 'eating' customers you would do well to consider this aspect.

It is also very useful to have one or two small areas which can be used for private parties. They can really help to boost trade, particularly when you are first starting up and in the evenings, if this is a quiet time. People come to the private functions and if they like the bar they may come back on their own or with friends. They may stay on for a meal and spend the whole evening with you.

Food, wine and service flow

Determining the flow of food, wine and services means looking in detail at the route each item takes from the service entrance to the point of purchase – bar or table. Draw up a simple plan of the premises and the way you are thinking of organising them. Then draw lines to represent the flow of all the items on sale. You may find that there are congestion points and you will need to check that there is sufficient space for you and your staff to do your designated jobs properly. Remember that items being cleared away should also go on the chart albeit in the opposite direction.

These deliberations should throw up the possibility of storage problems. Some premises have massive cellars and here the problem is one of strength in moving boxes rather than of space. But many other premises have very inadequate storage space. Do not forget that waste going out will also need to be stored for a while before it is collected.

It is also very easy to overlook the fact that you do not have anywhere for supply trucks to make deliveries or that there is an offending corner just asking to be removed. Careful plans for customer parking can also mean that the dustbin men cannot get at the refuse after 12 noon.

Customer flow

Another functional design consideration is the customer flow into and around the wine bar. How easy will it be to get to and from the service counters, can they get in and out of the toilet facilities easily and without fuss, and will they continually collide with service staff?

When David Nichols moved into Bubbles Wine Bar he completely changed the internal layout. The wine bar has a fairly long entrance which opens out at the back into an area about twice the width of the entrance. Behind that is a gallery for drinking and eating and the cellar stairs also descend from this area.

The previous owners of the wine bar had the bar itself situated along the side wall of the long narrow part of the room. This caused tremendous congestion as there were people coming to the bar to be served, and others standing there to eat and drink. Everyone going to or from the back area, the basement and the gallery had to pass through this already busy area.

In Bubbles the layout has the bar on the side of the large back area with plenty of waiting and standing space in front of it. The only other people passing through this area are those going up to the gallery. The front part is furnished with tables and chairs and the basement stairs go off before the bar is reached: all in all a much more sensible arrangement.

Problems can also occur if you have overflow areas without service points. In one large wine bar I visited in the south of England, you tended to lose your seat in the cellar if you went back to the upstairs bar for desserts or coffee.

In-built flexibility

Try to ensure that you build some flexibility into your operation so that you can change the menu or the method of serving without having to resort to more structural work and possible redecoration. It could be that your concept is spot on and success could push you up into a turnover double or treble that envisaged to start with. This could mean quite different systems.

Only after all these workaday factors have been taken into account and plans made to cope with them should you start thinking about decor in the sense of colour schemes, types of furniture, accessories, and bits and pieces generally. Once at this stage, however, theme and continuity are important. You will want to achieve a consistency of image in order to maximise visual impact. Everything the customer sees, feels and hears should be designed to convey the same message. All too often you will see an old-style building with a modern interior.

The last stage before work begins should be an evaluation process. This can be a most difficult time particularly if you like the final design, but you must try and put yourself in your potential customers' place and approach your projected wine bar as they might.

Will the place make a good first impression? Do the premises offer a warm and inviting environment, and is that environment right for them? As a customer, will you know immediately you walk through the door what is available and where to get it? Good staff can make customers feel welcome and point them in the right direction but you may not be employing many staff and at busy times you cannot always be in the right place to welcome new customers. Architectural and design guides help to sort things out.

Achieving an effect

Wine bar decors are as many and varied as their owners. There are Victorian wine bars with plush red upholstery and masses of paraphernalia, Dickensian bars with wooden panelling and plainer decor, wine vaults with exposed brick or stone-work, flagged floors and plenty of sawdust, and there are more modern designs with concrete, glass and lots of plants.

Some of these effects have been achieved by the expenditure of a good deal of money. Others have almost fallen together and slowly developed their atmosphere as the proprietor has picked up a few more bargains at the sale room.

What is certain is that your initial concept will probably be expensive and you may have to resign yourself to fulfilling only part of it to start with and then continuing to add to it as the money comes in. Indeed, a good many of the people I interviewed who had bought going concerns had spent the first year or so building up the business before redesigning or redecorating the premises. After all, value for money is more important than superficial frills and you do not need to spend the earth to get a reasonable effect.

If you are opening a new business you will have to start from scratch but you can save money by a little ingenuity and a lot of do-it-yourself. Of course, I am not suggesting that you should attempt any structural work yourself but fitting up can take a while and you could usefully fill that time by putting in some work of your own on the accessories.

James Walker of Wildes in Leamington Spa, for example, produced his own swan-neck light fittings. During the structural work on the premises the workmen removed lengths of old brass gas piping. Mr Walker polished them and

bent them into shape to make very
fittings. Pam and Allan Diamond of Te
Middlewich also carried out a good deal o   on
their bar themselves, including most of the
painting and decorating.

Sometimes the premises themselves have hidden potential. The Grapevine in Crediton had
originally been a pub and the panelling and
Victorian anaglypta ceiling were still in place.
Despite two winters of damp and neglect the proprietor and his father were able to save much of the
panelling and build in a bar to match.

Other buildings have revealed rough-cut stone
walls or attractive brick work underneath the
plaster, and flagstones have been discovered
under false floors. One owner in Oswestry uses the
old gas installations to light the bar. So look for
existing features before starting completely anew.

Accessories

The accessories can be just as important in
creating an atmosphere as the walls, floor and
colour scheme, and some of them can take a lot of
hunting down. Ideally, the overall impression
should be one of deliberate cohesion not a casual
conglomeration, though I have to say that in some
instances the latter works very well indeed.

The first essentials are the bar and bar stools
and the tables and chairs. The bar should be a
reasonable width but not so wide as to be
unfriendly and it will usually be made of wood,
though I saw one wine bar in Sussex which had a
most effective marble bar top. Another was made
of old railway sleepers.

Tables and chairs, too, are usually made of
wood. They may be purchased from outlets as
diverse as specialist furniture manufacturers and
government surplus sales. Others have come from
sale rooms and even newspaper advertisements;
some very attractive stained church pews were
found in just this way.

Pinewood furniture has been popular in some
wine bars and this, coupled with glass-top tables

and lots of plants, gives a lovely light and airy feel to the bar. In contrast is the hogshead table approach or converted treadle sewing machine tables and pub chairs. This type of decor relies heavily on candle light, usually in bottle holders, and plenty of wine racking and handmade oak casks or barrels around the place. The barrels can actually be used behind the bar to dispense sherry or boxed red wine. At Gales the proprietor saves money by making his own candles and recycling the used wax. Wine racking is often extended round the walls of the bar but these are best filled with empty bottles, partly for fear of theft but more importantly because the temperature in the bar will not be very good for the wine.

Other parts of the walls may be hung with posters or pictures. Posters are large and colourful and you can usually get something which will fit in with your own theme. You can also buy front-opening frames which can be fastened to the wall; they make poster changing quite easy and keep the posters in good condition for much longer than would be the case if they were put up with no protection at all.

Pictures can be expensive unless you manage to find a good job lot at a local sale. However, you could tie up with a local gallery or with local artists direct and sell original paintings or limited edition prints. In this way you could turn your walls into another profit centre. Richard Gale has done this to such good effect that his gallery business has extended to the rest of the house and turnover rivals that of the wine bar.

Photographs, particularly antique sepia-toned reproductions, offer another kind of wall covering. These are especially suited to wine bars with a nostalgic theme. Other wine bars use sporting prints, old maps or drawings of local landmarks, and one is completely decorated with heraldic insignia.

No wine bar is complete without chalkboards and very often the criterion is the more the better. This philosophy has its problems in that customers may miss something. On the other hand, a single large board can make the wine bar look a little too like a bistro. The answer lies in a combination of boards and printed wine list. The boards should carry the food menu, special offers and promotions such as a 'wine of the month' and details of bin ends and connoisseurs' wines. If you have a series of rooms or some pokey corners it is probably worth advertising desserts and coffee on extra boards in these areas, and perhaps port and brandy too. Do not forget that prices and menus also need to be displayed outside.

The subject of accessories must also cover all the glasses, crockery, cutlery and service items. If possible, it is good to choose all of these items so that they will be in keeping with the overall look in the wine bar but this is not always compatible with what is generally available and the problems of breakage and replacement. Remember, too, that some customers like to take 'souvenirs'.

Shopping list for accessories
Bar and bar stools
Tables and chairs
Other free-standing furniture for service and
    decoration
Coat and umbrella stands or hooks
Light fittings, candles and holders
Wine racking, barrels, casks and empty bottles
Pictures and posters
Chalkboards
Ornaments
Plants and plant-pot holders

Carafes, wine coolers and baskets
Glasses – preferably with the new measure
    mark line
Crockery and cutlery
Salt and pepper pots and other accessories
Food display platters, bowls etc
Corkscrews and bottle-opening equipment
Trays and clearing trolleys
Ashtrays, menu holders, flower holders etc
Table-cloths and napkins (linen or paper)

For specialist wine storage and cooking equipment see Chapters 8 and 9.

Music

In the planning stage it is worth considering whether or not you want music. This can be a quite expensive business for there is no point in installing inferior equipment which will only deliver rather scratchy sound. You will also have to pay a fee to the Performing Rights Society for permission to play records and tapes in a public place.

Some wine bar owners decide against music but it can be quite welcoming when the bar is only half full. If does stop that echoing sound which causes the first few customers to talk in subdued voices. However, you must pay attention to the sound levels you want. Customers may not like silence but there is nothing worse than not being able to hear yourself speak, and the staff have a tendency to turn the levels up to entertain themselves. By all means turn the levels up when the bar is full but do remember that some people are sitting by the speakers.

The type of music you play must, as usual, depend upon your clientele. Will they like classical music or are they strictly the popular music type? David Belford of Coolings told me that they play light classical music at lunch time and in the early evening, then, at about 8.30, they start to play popular music or have a live entertainer, for this is the time that the students from Exeter University start to congregate.

Live music can have quite a lot of drawing power but you do need a special entertainments licence. This subject is covered in more detail in Chapter 10.

Costumes and uniforms

Some wine bars attempt to carry their themes through to the waiters' and waitresses' costumes. This is very much a matter of personal preference and sometimes it does work. But staff are not usually keen to wear any kind of uniform however attractive and if, as proprietor, you decide to dress the part yourself, there is a danger of looking faintly ridiculous.

General facilities

In all the euphoria of planning the interior of the wine bar it is easy to forget that there is another essential area to be considered, namely the toilet facilities. Guides have been written to the best 'loos' in London or to loos in restaurants and these are not altogether frivolous. People do remember the toilet facilities – but usually only if they are very good or very bad.

To avoid the latter designation should not be too difficult. An attractively tiled area kept scrupulously clean and with plenty of soap, hot water, and clean towels or a hot air machine is all that is needed. Expenditure on this area is well worth the investment, but remember to add its upkeep to the top of the list of daily chores.

Other areas often overlooked are hanging facilities for possibly wet coats, the corridors through to the loos or to other private rooms and the staff areas. Staff areas need not be plush, but there must be some seating and a cheerful clean environment is better for morale than a drab and dingy area.

Where facilities are provided for the deposit of hats, coats, umbrellas etc on a hat stand or wall pegs, the licensee or wine bar owner may be liable for their loss. However, he can put up a conspicuous notice making it clear that articles are left at the owner's risk and that no responsibility is accepted by the wine bar for theft, loss or damage, however caused.

You will want somewhere to store vacuum cleaners and other cleaning materials and these will also need to be added to your list of initial equipment.

The exterior

The interior of your premises is probably more important than the exterior but do not write off the outside completely when you are making your redecoration budget. An attractive exterior can be a means of attracting customers and you certainly do not want people to pass by without really knowing you are there.

On the other hand, extensive changes will add considerably to the cost. The answer, of course, depends very much on the structure of your premises. One wine bar owner solved his particular problem by placing a screen of printed amber-coloured glass behind the existing window panes of his double shop frontage. The screening not only broke up the stark frontage, it also acted as double glazing and insulation against traffic noise.

Outside gardens or patios can be put to good use with a coat of white paint and some good garden furniture. Even in the British climate people like to sit outside, and evening barbecues can be a money-making operation during the summer months.

Chapter 7
The Wine List

The choice of wines for your initial list is vital to the success of the wine bar and the more time you can spend on planning it the better. After all, as Richard Gale of Llangollen put it, 'You only need to get it right once.' After that the same philosophy will dictate the choice of both replacement wines and new additions.

The first step, once again, is to return to your basic market research. Who will be your customers and what are their tastes likely to be? A small wine bar, for example, catering for young people in a residential area will not be able to sell the same wines as a city bar with a large business clientele. And a bistro-style wine bar will need something different again.

Nor is it any use thinking about the wines you personally like. If you are keen on wine these are likely to be far too expensive or too sophisticated for the majority of your customers. Remember that in any type of wine bar around 50 per cent of the customers will go for the house wine or for the half dozen least expensive wines on your list.

On the whole, people are not very adventurous in their choices and this is particularly true of wine where their knowledge may be somewhat limited. However, customers are looking for value for money, and serving inferior plonk on the basis that they will not know any better is a sure way to kill off your business.

Customers expect to be able to buy a pleasant wine without breaking the bank and they expect to be able to buy it more cheaply in a wine bar than in a restaurant. A good initial approach is to think in terms of providing good quality wines which are a

little different from those at the chain stores but
not much more expensive. Your customers will not
want to drink exactly the same wines as they drink
at home but will not want to pay through the nose
for the difference. Nor will they want to stray too
far away from the names that they know. All this
needs to be balanced against the price which you
will have to pay for the wine and the sort of mark-
up you can expect.

Deciding what to buy

Regardless of the way in which you finally decide
to present your wine list, the wines it will include
can be broken down into various categories. A
consideration of the content and balance of these
categories will be a great help in the final
compilation.

1. Style of wine by description
Start by looking at the style of wines that your
potential customers will expect to see on the list.
These will include:

Medium-dry white wines. Despite a trend towards
drier wines it is still true to say that the medium-
dry white wines are the most popular in Britain.
Very often these are represented by the German
wines on the list but there are also some excellent
mid-European wines which fall into this category
as well as some French wines.

Dry white. The choice here is extremely wide,
taking in many of the French, Italian and Spanish
wines. However, this is an area for experimenta-
tion and it might be worth trying out some of the
drier wines with a fruity flavour, such as Alsace
wines and the drier German wines, on the basis
that this is the kind of flavour expected in the
popular medium-dry category of wines, but with
much less sweetness. Portuguese Vinho Verde,
Tyrol wines and California wines also fit into this
category.

Sparkling wines. Special occasions call
thing a bit different and if you have a re
sparkling wine on offer it could be a best-
office parties and celebrations. At least ᴏᴜᴇ real
champagne is also essential for any list but do try
to offer a 'good buy' as well as the usual over-priced
well known brands. If you are likely to have a high
spending clientele you might consider a vintage
champagne.

Full-bodied red wines. Spanish and Italian wines
offer a good range of inexpensive full-bodied reds
but customers will also expect to see some French
wines included here. If your wine bar is in a potentially rich cosmopolitan area with a high degree of
well-to-do drinkers this and indeed other sections
of the list will also carry fine wines of vintage
quality. But even in this kind of location a good
slice of the business will come from relatively
inexpensive wine.

Dry red wines. Beaujolais is 'of course' the standby
here and since the very successful promotion of
Beaujolais nouveau some wine bars have made a
feature of both the *nouveau* and the *crus villages*.
But there are other less well known areas which
might be considered.

Rosé wines. Looking at some wine lists one might
be forgiven for wondering whether this category
needs to be included at all. But in fact some
customers do like rosé wine and there are one or
two which offer excellent value for money.

2. Different wine-producing areas
There are certain wine-growing areas which even
the least sophisticated wine drinker will expect to
see represented on your list. These include
Bordeaux, Burgundy and the Loire for France,
Hochheim (Hock) and Moselle for Germany and
Tuscany (Chianti), Orvieto, Soave and Valpolicella for Italy. There are of course many more wine
growing areas in these and in other countries and
you will need to consider which of them might

usefully be included. You will also need to balance familiar and unfamiliar wines, bearing in mind that to the new wine drinker Alsace wines, for example, may be a mystery while to the seasoned wine drinker they will be 'old hat'.

Most lists tend to concentrate on French wines with a smaller or larger sprinkling of wines from other countries, but there are some wine bar owners who have chosen to put the emphasis on German or Italian wines and there is even one wine bar in London specialising in Australian wines.

3. Different price ranges

Obviously, the prices of the wines on your list will be very important, and you will need to find the right balance of inexpensive, middle-price and costly wines. There tends to be a threshold somewhere around the £5 to £6 mark over which many customers will not usually go. The actual level varies in different parts of the country and in different socio-economic areas. You must therefore start by offering some wines whose price falls well below this level. These will probably be your house wines (see below), on sale by the glass or bottle.

The middle range of wines which fill the gap between the house wines and this sales threshold will form the majority of your list. In some areas you may decide that, apart from the odd bottle of champagne, you are unlikely to sell anything more expensive. But a cheap and cheerful wine list can still be quite extensive.

In other areas, there will be a small demand for fine wines which are more highly priced. These may form part of your regular list or you could fill the demand by buying bin ends and sales bargains, offering them as available. Most wine bar owners feel that a few really good wines enhance the reputation of their bars and some customers come especially for them. Others buy them to impress their friends or business associates.

The overall number of wines in each price category will depend on your storage space, how much capital you can afford to have tied up in this way, and on how adventurous and wide-ranging your customers will be. Some wine bars offer 100 or more wines. Others concentrate on a small list of interesting but inexpensive wines. The decision will depend on your judgement of the potential trade and how it might be developed.

4. House wines

With sales of house wines likely to account for 50 per cent or more of the bottles or glasses of wine sold in the bar, you must give particular attention to them. You cannot simply buy the cheapest wine going, as many bankrupt wine bar owners have discovered. Customers must feel confident that the house wine will be a pleasurable wine to drink. Indeed, for some, the first glass of house wine bought in your wine bar may be almost the first glass of wine ever and you must make sure it is not the last. One factor which really does stand out in differentiating the good wine bar from the bad is the number and quality of the house wines or of those wines which are available by the glass.

It is, of course, more difficult to ensure value for money at the lower end of the scale, particularly as there is quite a lot of bad wine on the market. But the house wine will be your bread and butter line and it must be able to stand on its own. It is important to shop around to get the best value. Very often the expenditure of a little more money will yield a disproportionately better wine. The lower profit margin will be offset by the greater sales and your customer will have much more confidence in you if the house wine is good. Indeed, care shown in this cheap end of the wine list is rightly taken to be indicative of the attitude taken throughout the list.

Once you start to study wine bar lists you will soon notice the great variation in the number of house wines on offer. Some bars simply have a red, white and a rosé house wine, perhaps with a few others offered by the glass. Others offer as many as a dozen or more different house wines ranging up into the middle-price wines. To my mind, the latter approach shows much more concern for the customer who can try out possibly unfamiliar wines without having to commit himself to a bottle. It's a long-sighted approach, too, for the chances are that at least some customers will order a bottle the next time they come in.

House wine will usually have the bottler's or shipper's label on it but it is perfectly possible for you to have your own label. However, the label is legally bound to provide certain information: first of all the label must say 'Table Wine'. This can be given in any language of the European Economic Community, and will usually be in the language of the country of origin. This country of origin must also be stated on the label. The word 'reserve' must not be used unless the wine is an *appellation contrôlée* wine or equivalent. The size of the bottle and the name of the bottler must also be shown, but this name must not be more than half the size of the words 'Table Wine'. This stops the bottle looking too grand and the wine possibly being passed off for something better than it is. You may, of course, give the name of the wine bar and this can be as large as you like. For more information on the EEC regulations about the labelling of wines, check with the Wine Standards Board in London.

Sample wine lists
Here are four typical wine lists gathered from a variety of quite different types of wine bar. I have left out the actual vintages and prices as these obviously change from time to time.

AC = *Appellation contrôlée*
DOC = *Denominazione di Origine Controllata*
FB = French bottled
QbA = *Qualitätswein bestimmter Anbaugebiete*

1. This list is taken from a small London wine bar in a residential and tourist area. It concentrates on inexpensive wines and apart from the champagne,

there is nothing priced over £7. There is a good selection of food ranging from snacks to full meals. *House wines also available by the glass.

French red wine
Domaine du Parc*
Le Piat d'Or*

Red Bordeaux
Bordeaux Rouge FB
Château de Marsan AC

Red Burgundy
Bourgogne – Croix St
  Louis FB

French white wine
Domaine les Milles*
Le Piat d'Or

White Bordeaux
Bordeaux Blanc
Bergerac Blanc

White Burgundy
Mâcon Villages FB

Loire
Vouvray Cuvée Haut
  Renommée
Muscadet de Sèvre et
  Maine FB

Rhône
Côte du Rhône

Rosé
Anjou Rosé

Germany
Liebfraumilch QbA
Niersteiner Gutes
  Domtal
Piesporter Michelsberg
Bereich Bernkastel

Italy
Valpolicella Classico
  Superiore DOC
Bardolino DOC*
Soave DOC*
Frascati Secco DOC

Portugal
Vinho Verde

Sparkling wines
Freixenet (Spanish,
  medium)
Chanderelle Cordon
  D'Argent

Champagne
Lambert – Extra Dry
Moët & Chandon

Also port, sherry, brandy and lager and a selection of seven cocktails

2. This is the list of an inner city wine bar with a business clientele at lunch time plus a good evening trade. The food is all cold and fairly straightforward.

*Available by the glass.

White wine	*Red wine*
French White 'Ordinary' No 1 (dry)*	French Red 'Ordinary'*
	House Claret AC*
Best Bordeaux Sauvignon*	House Rioja*
Pinot Blanc d'Alsace*	Côte du Rhône, Château de l'Estagnel
Pouilly Vinzelles Vintage	Beaujolais Villages
Mâcon Blanc Villages	Clos de Cent Jours, Côtes de Blaye
Davy's Muscadet 'Sur Lie' Domaine de l'Augerie	Côte de Brouilly
	Davy's St Julien
House Moselle*	Château Bellegrave, Pauillac
House Hock*	Château Lagrange, St Julien

Rosé	*Champagne*
Anjou Rosé	Veuve Clicquot*
	Krug Vintage

Plus sherry, port and cognac.

3. This list comes from a medium-sized general wine bar situated in an attractive market town in the Midlands. The food offered includes hot and cold meals and is fairly elaborate. In the evenings the bar is used both as a wine bar and as a restaurant.
*Available by the glass.

House wine	*Rosé*
Arc de Triomphe, red and white*	Anjou Rosé
	Mateus Rosé

Red Burgundy	*Alsace*
Côte de Villages Rouge*	Gewürztraminer
Mâcon Rouge AC	*Austria*
Beaujolais AC*	Schluck
Comtes de Chartogne AC Bourgogne	
	Italy
Château de Fleurie	Soave DOC
Nuits Saint Georges	Valpolicella DOC
Gevrey Chambertin	Frascati Secco

White Burgundy
Côtes de Villages,
 Beaune*
Chablis AC
Pouilly Fuissé

Red Bordeaux
Roi de France Claret*
Médoc AC
Saint Emilion AC
Château Bellevue AC
Château Latour
 Camblanes
Château le Loup

White Bordeaux
Graves AC
Sauternes AC

Rhône
Côtes du Rhône AC
Cuvée de Rocheline

Loirs
Caves Membrolle
Vouvray
Muscadet

Romania
Traminer

Yugoslavia
Lutomer Riesling

Rhine
Hock Motzart
Liebfraumilch*
Bereich Nierstein
Johannisberger
 Riesling

Moselle
Moselblümchen Blue
 Crest
Piesporter
 Goldtröpfchen
Bernkastel Riesling

Champagne
Jules Mernier
Ayala
Moët & Chandon

Sparkling wines
Club Prestige, dry and
 medium sweet*

Also three ports and three brandies, plus sherry,
beer and lager.

4.   This is part of the list of a wine bar which is one
of the three in a first-class group of London-based
wine bars. Prices vary from £4 to £26 but the
average price is nearer £6 to £7. The food is mainly
of the cold buffet type and the bar is busy at lunch
time and in the evening.

House wines (all avail-
 able by the glass)
La Fleuralie, Blanc and
 Rouge
Liebfraumilch

Sparkling Brut Duc
 D'Ordy
Sauvignon de Touraine
Alsace Pinot Blanc
Mâcon Blanc, Domaine
 des Roches

Beaujolais, Domaine la Combe

Claret Château Charron, Côtes de Bourg

Rioja, Marqués de Caceras

Champagne, Joseph Perrier

Sparkling house wines
Jean Perico (Spanish)
Crémant de Bourgogne Rosé
Blanquette de Limoux

French wines:
Alsace
Pinot Blanc
Riesling
Muscat
Gewürztraminer (2)

Loire
Sauvignon de Touraine
Muscadet de Sèvre et Maine
Pouilly Blanc Fumé
Sancerre

White Bordeaux
Château Saint Armand, Sauternes
Château Brouslet, Barsac

Red Bordeaux
Château Charron, Côtes de Bourg
La Mouline
Domaine de Gaillat, Graves
Château La Grombande, Margaux

Château La Garde, Graves
Château Millet, Graves
Château Marsac, Margaux
Château Pichon, Pauillac
Château Figeac, Saint Emilion
Château Cheval Blanc

White Burgundy
Mâcon Blanc
Mâcon Chardonnay
Chablis Labonne Roi
Domaine Réné Manuel, Bourgogne Blanc
Meursault (2)

Red Burgundy
Bourgogne Davenay
Givry, Côte Challonais
Fixin, Côte de Nuits
Mercurey
Côtes de Nuits Village
Santenay
Beaune Theurons
Beaune Clos des Mouches
Chambolle Musigny Les Charmes

Beaujolais
Beaujolais Blanc Château de Châtelard
Beaujolais Villages Domaine la Combe
Hospices de Beaujolais la Plaigne
Morgon Domaine de Vieux Cèdres
Brouilly Grand Clos de Briante

Chiroubles
Moulin-à-Vent, de la
  Bruyère
Robin Chenas,
  Domaine de Brureaux

Rhône
Domaine de Fontsarde
Vacqueryas
Crozes-Hermitage
Châteauneuf du Pape

Provence
Château Grand Sevil

Rosé
Château Grand Sevil
  Rosé
Domaines Ott Château
  de Selle

Germany
Selection of five Moselle
  wines and six hocks

Spain
Selection of three red
  wines and one white

Italy
Selection of three white
  wines and four red

New Zealand
Selection of three wines

English wine
Abbey Knight

California
Selection of two red
  wines and two white

Australia
Selection of seven
  wines

Champagne
10 different
  champagnes ranging
  from £9.95 to £25

Even from this small taste of the wine lists on offer you can see what very big differences there are in the market. Before you start to map out your own wine list have a look at the lists of as many wine bars as you can, but be sure they have a similar catchment area to yours. Try to judge how successful they are. Next, write an outline list indicating the different types of wine which ought to be included, their number and price and quality range. Do not be too rigid in your ideas at this stage. It could be that when you start to shop around for the wine, one variety of a particular type of wine may offer better value than another. Or you may come across an area which is new to you but which offers the right sort of wine at the right price.

Where to buy

You should now have a clear idea of what sort of
wine you are looking for, but where are you going
to buy it? There are, after all, hundreds of wine
merchants and shippers from which to choose.
There is also the possibility of buying at least some
of your wine direct from the growers or *négociants*
in France or elsewhere. In the first instance,
however, it makes sense to build up a relationship
with one or more home-based suppliers. It's all
very well to think of dashing off to France and
bringing home 20 dozen cases of wine in the van,
planning no doubt to top up with bin ends and
bargain parcels. A successful wine bar simply
cannot be started and run in such a haphazard
way. There has to be an element of reason
somewhere!

If you are serious about wanting to buy some of
your wine direct, bide your time. Learn about the
areas in which you are particularly interested and
start to build up contacts. In the meantime you will
need to stock up here.

UK merchants and shippers

The choice of UK-based merchants and shippers
ranges from the big companies such as Grants of
St James and Stowells through chains like
Victoria Wine and Peter Dominic to smaller more
specialist shippers such as Reynier and Dolamore.
Some of these companies are London based, others
have branches throughout the provinces. There
are also some very good smaller companies based
in towns and cities all over the country.

At first glance the big company route looks as
though it may be a little restricting but it does have
some advantages and quite a number of very
independent-minded owners do buy the majority
of their wines from companies like Grants of St
James. They can, of course, also buy wines from
other shippers, though the big companies tend to
discourage this on the basis that owners should
consider the advantage of the big brand image

which also offers other less well known wines not available in the supermarkets. The big companies can help in the production of wine lists, point of sale aids such as ice buckets, wine maps and roll-up blackboards, and in promotional ideas to increase sales.

Certainly the big companies can offer reasonably good wines at the most competitive prices and if your customers are likely to be buying solely on price this could be very important. Working with one or two major suppliers gives continuity and also takes some of the constant decision making away from you. They have the most up-to-date information on market trends and can keep you informed on what is happening in similar bars elsewhere.

If, however, you are likely to have customers who want to take more of an interest in wines generally you may decide to shop around and buy from a number of different shippers. Here the pattern varies from one wine bar to another. Some owners like to deal with London-based shippers and others opt for the local companies. Remember, too, that some shippers are very good in one area but may not be so good with wines from elsewhere. Allan Diamond of Tempters buys his unusual list from a variety of companies.

Nigel Ravenshill of Wheels Wine Bar in Barnstaple, on the other hand, told me that he had started out buying, mainly by telephone, from London but that after one or two changes he had moved his business to a couple of locally based firms. He believes that the personal contact he now has with his suppliers has been good for the business. He pays COD and has been able to negotiate keener prices. In addition, his suppliers know his business and have come up with their own suggestions for a new house wine or a bin-end bargain for the chalkboards.

This sort of interaction can be very important when time is at a premium. Another owner based in the Midlands agreed that the local supplier was the best as far as he was concerned. At the planning stage he had imagined himself gently drifting round Europe and buying, where possible, direct from growers. By the time the wine bar opened this idea had dwindled to the decision to shop around in the UK to find the best buys for each section of his list. Some three years later he told me that although he does spend quite a lot of time poring over lists to check quality and cost he deals in the main with only three suppliers. Because he is very caught up in the day-to-day running of the bar, he is dependent on their representatives bringing him news of quality changes in the range and bin-end bargains. His personal relationship with the reps means that he feels he can trust them.

Of course, when you are first starting up you do not have any special relationships and you may not be sure just who are likely to be the right suppliers. Start by talking to as many as possible and listen carefully to what they have to say. Judith Rose of Boos Wine Bar in London says that wine bar owners should beware of people selling wine who start by telling you how reasonable the wine is, then go on to tell you how well presented it is and finally tell you how good the quality is. The order should be the other way round!

All the merchants and shippers, however honest, are going to push their own wines. Some of them really will be the best, but the judgement is up to you and the more you can learn about wines the better able you will be to make these decisions.

Buying direct

If you are determined to buy at least some of your wine direct do not be too discouraged by those owners who have dropped by the wayside. There are some very successful wine bar owners in London and elsewhere who buy between 60 and 80 per cent of their wine direct from the countries of origin. The secret is to take your time. Do not rush into it in a big way until you are sure you know what you are doing. The problem is, of course, that there are just so very many wines to choose from. It is even more important, therefore, to build up an in-depth knowledge of wine and this includes tasting as well as reading and talking to experts. You cannot hope to become an expert in all wines without many years of study. Start by choosing one or two growing areas of the wine which you think will appeal to your customers and concentrate on these.

You do not necessarily have to leave the UK to buy direct but holidays spent in France or one of the other wine growing countries (if you have decided to specialise there) will be a great help in trying the wine on the spot and meeting the growers and bottlers.

Read all the books you can find and take out subscriptions to magazines like *Harpers Wine and Spirit Trade Gazette* and *Decanter*. Go to as many tastings as possible. To find out about these, look in the magazines and write to the major shippers from your areas of interest. They hold regular wine tastings, as do national promotional bodies such as Food and Wine from France and the German Wine Information Service. These tastings enable you to judge the quality of the different wines for yourself and will enable you to talk with much more authority to your customers.

You also will meet other people from the wine trade at these tastings, and at the larger functions you will have the opportunity to taste a very wide range of wines without ever leaving the country. Very often the producers themselves will be there and you can make contacts which could have taken you many weeks of travelling. Remember, too, that wine shippers like Deinhards, Hallgartens, Reynier and Sichel will all organise ex-cellar sales for a small commission. There are also some shippers such as Beaumont and Richmond who devote as much as half their wine list to direct buying offers.

Buying direct can raise the question of special documentation and bonding. This is taken care of if you buy from a specialist shipper but if you are making your own arrangements with the grower you will need to find your own shipping company. In fact this is not as daunting as it sounds. Look in the Yellow Pages for companies like P & O and Seabrook & Smith which have special sections to deal with wine consignments. If you get the right shipping company they will take all the administration off your shoulders. All you have to do is place an order with the supplier and send a copy to the shipper.

As always, shopping around pays off. First of all you will want to compare the actual rates. Shippers' rates vary at the smaller end of their scales. Remember that 50 cases of wine may be a large order to you but it is peanuts to a company like P & O who probably ship for the big merchants. Watch out, too, for the fact that one shipping company may be very reasonable on wines from certain areas but more expensive from others.

The time factor comes into it too. One shipper may be offering a low price but take longer to deliver than another, because one company has a depot in the area and the other has not. Some companies may also be able to arrange part loads or groupage and others may not. In this connection it is worth considering combining with other wine bars for a larger order.

Check too, that the prices cover the administration. A good shipper will actually chase the grower for you and you will not be faced with the possibility of having to make phone calls in a foreign language. They will let you know when the wine can be expected at the bond stores. Find out in advance where the bond stores are. You do not want to have to drive long distances to collect the wine or to pay further delivery costs. Judith and Michael Rose now buy over 75 per cent of their wines direct. They keep them in bond in Kennington and simply draw 25 cases from time to time on their way to work from their home in Streatham. This method avoids both delivery and storage problems.

Buying direct can mean a larger investment in

wine than you would have to make buying regularly from a UK merchant, but it can pay off. After all, you are cutting out the middleman and if you get the timing right you will have sold a fair percentage of it before you have to pay the supplier. You will usually have between 30 and 45 days from the date of shipment to settle the bill and this may be extended to 60 days when the supplier gets to know you or when you are buying from the 'newer' wine countries such as Australia, Portugal, Spain and South Africa. This time lapse means that you can tell your bank to take advantage of the most favourable rate of exchange during the payment period.

Even if you are buying from a specialist wine merchant and shipper, his prices for this type of business will be based on the cost of wine in the European cellars and the shipper's low prices will allow you to take a wider margin yourself.

Customs duty, shipping and insurance will have to be paid immediately as there is rarely any credit period allowed on these payments. However, if you have the wine transferred directly on landing to a bonded warehouse in your own name, you will not have to pay the customs duty until you want to move it into your own cellars.

Perhaps, more importantly, buying direct means having the opportunity to buy the very best in each price range from a region rather than pay the merchant a premium for possibly inferior wines. If you get it right you can keep the same margins and offer a very good wine. Steve Jones in Southend buys his wine direct and says that he could buy wine up to £5 a case cheaper. However, he believes that it is not worth it as, in the long run, he would lose customers to other bars if he let his standards slip.

Other wine bar owners like Richard Gale and the Roses also add to their profits by selling their own directly bought wine to other wine bars or to customers.

How much wine to stock?

If you are buying wine direct you will usually have to take more than if you are buying in the UK, but there is no reason why you should not mix the two methods.

By and large, the decision on how much wine to buy will depend upon the capacity of the wine bar, the storage space and the amount of capital you can afford to have tied up in stock.

In the early stages it is difficult to know exactly how much wine your customers will consume in any given period. You know that you can cater for, say, 50 people but you will have to make a calculated guess about whether or not you will be full in the evenings, and about your customers' buying patterns generally. It is better to slightly over-order to start with, as nothing looks worse in a relatively new wine bar than wines which are crossed off the list or are unavailable when requested. However, after a period of operating a daily or weekly stock check, you will be in a better position to see what needs to be replaced and when.

Storage space is much easier to calculate. You can simply measure the walls, install the racking and count the holes! If storage space is difficult you can hold stocks on visible display round the walls of the bar. Perhaps not always the best temperature conditions, but at least in one northern bar, the owner's wife has a little more space to work in the back kitchen.

If money is tight, buying in a large amount of stock is likely to mean more interest to pay and, in today's climate of relatively high interest rates, this can be expensive. Money tied up in stock can also cause cash flow problems. Operating on a fairly low stock level has the advantage, too, of helping you to avoid expensive mistakes. If you have ordered only a small amount of a particular new wine you will have less of a problem realising your money if it is not too popular.

Regular stock checks and a good relationship with your supplier should ensure continuity. There may, however, be a case to be made for buying in larger quantities of a particular wine if you can get it at a good price and know it to be popular. A private wine lake may not be sensible but the odd well bought pool can be a money-maker and a customer-keeper!

Pricing the wine

You need to be very clear about the basis on which your prices are fixed. If you are not you will find it very difficult to work out even the initial estimates for your business. Some wine bar owners have started off by saying to themselves, 'I am going to charge as much as I can get,' or more conservatively, 'I am going to charge what other wine bars charge in similar situations.' Both of these approaches are fine as far as they go and they could perhaps provide a reasonable starting-off point, but at some stage you will be wondering whether you should put prices up or even if you should reduce them to attract more business. It is at this point that you need to know exactly what costs you are trying to cover and what your profit margins really are.

It could be that a similarly priced wine bar down the road is buying all its wine direct and is thus able to make a better profit than you can buying from your London merchant. Or the rent may be lower than your new lease. On the face of it, charging more than the opposition may not seem like a very good idea, but if you are offering better food or a more interesting wine list you should be able to get away with it.

Getting the pricing right is very important in a business like a wine bar. The sale is not a one-off job where it might not matter too much if the customer does not return. You need your customers to keep on coming back for more.

Obviously your prices need to cover the cost of the wine to you, but they also need to contribute not only towards any other variable costs such as wages and fuel but also to fixed overheads such as interest, rent and rates. And after all of this has been paid for there is your own or the company's profit to think about.

In the first instance you will have to estimate your costs. For the variable costs you will have to make a judgement on how many people you are likely to serve at lunch time and how many in the evening, how much they are likely to spend and on what. Fixed costs are a little easier to estimate. Interest rates you will know and you can find out levels for rent and rates.

From these estimates you will be able to work out, on average, how many bottles of wine you would expect to sell in a week. This can then be set against the projected volume of costs. To give a simple example: if you expect to sell 100 bottles of wine which cost you £2 each, your first variable cost will be £200. If the rest of your variable and fixed costs including your own remuneration came to a further £400 you would have to charge £6 per bottle. However, you will also be selling food, so some of the overheads can be apportioned to this sector bringing the cost of your bottle down to £5 or so.

This sort of calculation will give you a basis on which to set your prices. Of course, in practice things are a bit more complicated than this. Once you have been operating for a time you will be able to replace estimated costs with actual costs and this will give you a much more accurate calculation. The first basis for your calculations must be the house wine – the majority of your sales are going to come from this. Quite a number of wine bar owners use the above type of calculation to give them a percentage mark-up from which to work. In the simple example given above the percentage mark-up would be 150, which percentage would be added to the base cost of every bottle of wine sold.

However, there are pitfalls with this approach, particularly at the more expensive end of your price range. This kind of mark-up would mean that a bottle of wine costing you £4 would have to be priced at £10, considerably above the threshold for most wine bars and the problem gets progressively worse if you are planning to sell fine vintage wines or good champagne.

Another way of looking at it would be to say, from the original calculation, that the cash mark-up must be £3 to cover all costs. By this calculation the £4 bottle of wine would be charged at £7.

In reality neither calculation is very sensible. It is arguable that the £7 price loses you £3 *but* this is true only if you are sure that the bottle will sell at £10. The chances are that it will not. It will merely sit in the cellars tying up money which could be used elsewhere. The most sensible solution is to price the bottle experimentally somewhere between the two, say £8.50. If it sells you are £1.50 better off than with either of the other prices and if it doesn't sell you can adjust the price again. A review every three months or so will show you what is and what is not selling and a change in the pricing policy could make all the difference.

Presenting and serving wines

Obviously the first thing that customers entering a wine bar want to know is what wines are available. Indeed, the question of informing customers what you have to offer should start outside the wine bar. The law requires you to display a representative selection of wines for potential customers to see without coming inside at all.

Once they are inside, you want to convey as much information as you can in the shortest possible time. There are various ways of doing this, such as printed, typed or handwritten wine lists, chalkboards and table cards. Most wine bars use a mixture of these but there are very few which do not use at least one chalkboard.

Chalkboard or wine list?
Chalkboards have come to be a symbol of the wine bar atmosphere. In some bars there are as many as eight or ten boards dotted about the walls, on the

bar top or propped up against some barrels. Some of these boards carry the same information so that every part of the bar is equally well informed on the wine available.

Very often there will be one large board listing the majority of the wines the establishment has to offer. This will be supplemented by boards listing 'the wine of the month' or any special offers, fine wines and bin-ends, port and brandy prices and anything else the proprietor wants to push. Chalkboards have the advantage of being very easy to change and many wine bars do change their lists once or twice a year, but unless a board is devoted to a single wine there is very little room to give much information about the wine.

A wine list, on the other hand, has much more potential. If it is typed or handwritten it can be changed quite easily, but this can look a little tatty. Bubbles and its sister wine bars have partially solved this problem by using an attractive style of handwriting and by laminating the outside four pages.

A printed wine list gives some authority to the list but it can be expensive. Small print runs mean high cost but longer print runs mean that changes will have to be made by hand and if you are not careful the list can end up looking just as messy as a badly handwritten one.

Of course, part of this problem can be solved by including only wines which are likely to be around for some time and by leaving the producer, vintage and price detail area blank to be filled in by hand. This type of list can be supplemented with details of shorter term special offers and fine wines set out on the inevitable chalkboards.

How much information?
The questions of what information to include on a wine list and how the wine should be arranged are less easy to answer than they seem. Some lists are extremely vague about the wines, others are full of jargon. Of course, some customers want to know 'chapter and verse' about the shippers or *négo-*

ciants, the specific quality of the wine and where it comes from. Others are quite simply confused by too much information and will become even more securely attracted to the house wine than they were before. Even worse, if they are completely overawed, they may not come back at all.

So once again we are back to answering the question: what kind of wine bar are you setting up? Who are the clients likely to be and what will they want to know? If the answer includes a high percentage of customers who are not likely to know too much about wine it may pay off to arrange the wine list in a completely different way from the traditional grouping by country. Stowells, for example, have produced lists for establishments which list wine by style so that customers wanting dry white wine, medium white, full red or whatever can make a quick choice without embarrassment.

Allan Diamond of Tempters believes that his customers mostly buy on price and to make it easy for them he has quite simply arranged his list in price order. Each wine has a short write-up on where it comes from, its style and where appropriate, appellation and vintage details. If, however, your wine bar is likely to be serving people with a greater knowledge, or pretentions to knowledge, you may want to stick with the traditional approach.

However you decide to arrange your wine list, it is important to give as much information as possible. Customers are much more likely to try unfamiliar wines or wines with unpronounceable names if they can gain some idea of what they will be like. And please do explain what abbreviations such as AC, FB or DOC mean. Ideally, you or your staff should be the main source of information on your wines. This word-of-mouth education is both painless and pleasant and is the best way of getting customers to be a little more adventurous in their choice of wines. Unfortunately, you do not always have time to talk to everyone.

One answer to lack of space is to choose four or five wines from the list each month and designate them 'Wines of the Month'. Use a typed or hand-written insert to give more information about these wines than is usually possible. This can be backed up with chalkboard advertising, a special price, and the offer of wine by the glass on wines which are not normally sold in this way. If you are buying from one of the big suppliers such as Grants of St James they will usually be able to supply this kind of material ready printed.

This sort of technique helps to educate your customers and it gives them the chance to try wines they might not otherwise drink. Too often timid customers stick to the house wines and do not realise that for the very small extra charge on other wines they will be getting even better value for money. The technique also helps you to increase the range of wines you sell and thus the profit contributed by the wine sector of your business.

Wines by the glass, carafe and half bottle
Some owners maintain that it is not worth offering a large range of wines by the glass because only the house wines are chosen and the others remain open but untouched. Other owners, however, have popularised a much wider range of wines by featuring them in the type of promotions outlined above and as a result have also extended the range of bottles ordered.

The actual sizes of glasses which you may use in a wine bar are outlined in Chapter 4. The choice is reasonably large and it is important to choose the right size or sizes for your location. If you have customers who pop in for a quick glass of wine you may find that the larger sizes are too big. On the other hand, customers who want to sit for a while may find the smaller ones insufficient.

The psychological aspect also needs to be considered. Small glasses can seem to the customer to be very reasonably priced but they may also appear to empty very quickly, necessitating frequent refills over a couple of hours or so. This might be seen as good for the owner but bad for the customer.

Large glasses on the other hand, though obviously more expensive, appear much more generous. They last much longer and if the customer does buy a refill he does not feel he has had to do so too soon. This system is good for the owner too, as the second large glass, quite happily bought, brings a greater profit than the second smaller glass.

You can, of course, try to have your cake and eat it by offering two sizes of glass. Remember that you will need to state the actual sizes so that the customer can work out the price per decilitre.

If part of your reason for serving a fairly large selection of wines by the glass is to interest your customer in a wider range, you will want to make sure that these wines are in peak condition. This can be difficult when you do not know precisely how much is going to be drunk.

There is slightly less worry with the red wines as most of these will benefit from being open for a while before they are served.

White wines cause rather more of a problem as they need to be kept chilled. The variety of bar fixtures which will keep wine chilled at the right temperature range from chill boxes with bar optics, probably not very appropriate in a wine bar, to attractive 'tubs' which stand on the bar top and will hold up to seven or eight bottles at a time.

You will also need to have some sort of bottle chilling unit in the bar area and this can also be used to keep opened bottles cool. Sherries and tawny ports will keep for much longer than wine in opened bottles, but there are differences. Fino sherry, for example, will not keep for longer than a week and should be kept chilled. Oloroso, on the other hand, will keep for much longer.

In some wine bars the house wine is served in carafes rather than bottles and though this does mean that there are quantities available in sizes between the glass and the full bottle, it can also look as though you are trying to do the customer down in some way. The customer is probably justified in this view since the chances are that you are serving boxed rather than bottled wine. There is nothing intrinsically wrong in this but the customer should be told exactly what he is drinking and how it is packaged.

The subject of half bottles is also worth considering here. Very few wine bars offer any half bottles at all and this can be very annoying for the customer who wants to drink a better wine than the house wine but does not want to consume a whole bottle.

The usual answer to a complaint about the lack of half bottles is that they are not available. This is not strictly true. There may be difficulties in some areas but the truth of the matter usually is that the owner does not want to be bothered with them. However, if you take this attitude you could lose potential customers. One alternative might be to offer such customers the opportunity to have a bottle and to pay only for the amount drunk.

One wine bar owner in Sussex is prepared to take this course on the basis that it did not happen very often, and when it did the customer often ended up drinking the full bottle. Even if he didn't, the gain in goodwill offset the loss on the bottle which was usually polished off by the owner later in the day. Another solution is to offer one or two better wines by the glass.

Storage and stock control

By and large your storage facilities will be dictated by the premises you acquire but where possible, factors of temperature, single-row stacking and ease of access should be taken into consideration and do try not to under-estimate what your cellarage requirements will be – many prospective owners do and then have a headache trying to find a place for all the wine.

The better planned your wine cellar, the easier it will be to run this part of your business. A mass of wine cases stacked haphazardly in the cellar is bound to lead to chaos and is an open temptation to pilfering on a possibly large scale.

Ideally you should plan your cellar with separate areas or 'bins' for each wine on the list and with extra space for fine wine bargains, new wines and those you might be trying out in small quantities experimentally. Make sure that the bins for house wines and other potentially popular wines are large enough to take the sort of expanded stocks you may need at Christmas time.

Label each bin with the full details of the wine and make out a stock control card which can also be pinned to the bin. This card should show the date the wine came in and the quantity. Further sections will show the dates that wine is removed, the quantities which are taken out and, if you have two or more bars, its destination.

Here's a sample card from which to work:

Stock Control Card

Description MOUTON CADET Selection Baron Rothschild 1978					
Date	*Existing stock and deliveries in*	*Cellar Bar*	*Issues out* *Ground Floor Bar*	*Total*	*Balance*
1.9.83	24 (+consignment number)				24
4.9.83		2	1	3	21
6.9.83		1		1	20
8.9.83		1	4	5	15
9.9.83	12		1	1	26

Records might be kept daily, as in the example, or they could be kept on a weekly basis.

The value of this sort of stock control card is that you can see at a glance whether a particular wine needs to be re-ordered. It makes stocktaking easy and you also have a check on where each bottle of wine has gone. These records can be checked against the bar tallies and certain kinds of fiddling by the bar staff will become immediately apparent.

You should also take care checking stocks into your cellars. Be on hand when deliveries are made and personally count and check every case.

Getting rid of the empties

Empty bottles can be a major headache in a wine bar. There is, after all, a limit to the number of dusty empties you can use for wall decoration or for holding candles. The rest have to be stored somewhere until the binmen collect them or until you are able to take them to a bottle bank.

If you have a sheltered area in a backyard or an unused outhouse you can keep the wine boxes as they come in and use them to hold the empties for collection. However, you must not take it for granted that the local authority will automatically remove your bottles or any other kind of refuse. The usual weekly service will probably be inadequate and you may have to make special arrangements for a more frequent collection. Talk to your local authority first and see what they can offer. Services do vary tremendously in different parts of the country. Alternatively, you may have to make arrangements for a private waste disposal company to collect from you.

In this connection the Glass Manufacturers' Federation have a list of special merchants who operate cullet (waste glass) schemes around the country. There are also a number of bottle banks operated by local authorities. These are huge skips to which you can take your bottles, but their use can be time consuming as the banks may be some distance away and, since they are designed with private individuals in mind, you have to sort and feed the bottles in one by one!

Chapter 8
The Menu

Nowadays the food served in a wine bar is almost as important as the wine and it is even more difficult to determine what makes good wine bar food than to decide what the wines should encompass. Wine bars up and down the country offer an extremely varied selection of food and it is not easy to define exactly how the successful ones achieve their results.

However, a high standard of cooking and attention to detail, coupled with value for money, are certainly very important. This holds good as much for a bar serving jacket baked potatoes, cold side salads and quiche as it does for those specialising in expensive steaks or offering almost restaurant-like menus. In all cases good home-style cooking seems to be the order of the day. Chefs are conspicuous by their absence but so is bought-in food.

A study of potential customers seems, on the surface, to be less important here than the style and atmosphere of the wine bar. Certainly those wine bars frequented by busy shoppers or young people do not offer such elaborate food as those situated in wealthy residential areas but this kind of distinction is not very marked. Wine bars with quite simple wine lists can and do offer and sell fairly expensive dishes alongside their snacks and salads. On the other hand, some wine bars with extensive and possibly expensive wine lists offer relatively simple food and in the middle there are those who seem to offer something of everything!

It could be that the research needed to establish a successful pattern of food should be focused not only on the potential customer but also on what is or is not available elsewhere in the area. Add to this your own view of good food, and on top of it all, consider the skills of your cook. Very often the cook is the proprietor's wife and even if she is not planning to do the cooking herself she will probably be deeply involved in menu planning and supervision. If the cook enjoys what he or she is doing, and is good at it, the end result will be far better than when the cooking is to a pre-set pattern.

Typical wine bar menus

Here are some examples of menus taken from wine bars in various parts of the country.

1. This menu is taken from a large city wine bar which has an extensive wine list priced only a little above the house wine. At the time of my visit, with the exception of champagne, there were no wines priced over £7. The menu is the same at lunch time and in the evening.

Hot food
Lentil Soup
Cottage Pie with Red Cabbage
Lasagne
Macaroni Cheese
Vegetable Risotto
Aubergine Provençal

Cold food
*The word 'dip' refers to the salad section

Chicken Waldorf ⎫
Spiced Ham and Egg ⎬ Price includes
Tuna and Rice Salad ⎭ two side salads
Egg, Vegetable and
  Cheese Platter
4 Dip Main Course Selection*
Sugar Baked Ham and Salad
Roast ½ Chicken and Salad
Quiche and Salad
Chicken Liver Pâté and Bread

Curried Eggs and Salad
Smoked Mackerel
Rollmop Herrings
Side Salad Selection (2 Dips) *

Sweets etc
Cheesecake
Lemon Meringue and Cream
Syrup Tart and Cream
Black Cherry Chiffon and Cream
Belgian Fudge Cake

Cheeses
Coffee

2. This is the lunch-time menu from a bistro-style wine bar situated in a small country town in the south west. All the places are usually booked ahead.

Home-made Soup
Pâté au Poivre
Smoked Fish Pâté
Stuffed Advocado

Spiced Grilled Chicken
Beef in Red Wine
Chicken and Spinach Lasagne
Beef Stroganoff

Home-made Ice Cream:
Honey and Brandy, Coffee and Walnut
Cheese and Biscuits

The menu is expanded somewhat in the evenings to include items such as salmon pâté, fresh asparagus, and mushrooms in cream and brandy among the starters; roast duck, peppered sirloin steak and pork with apricots among the main courses and raspberry shortcake, chocolate rum basque and blackberry mousse among the desserts.

3. This evening menu comes from a good all-round wine bar in the Midlands. The wine list ranges from a good but inexpensive house wine to

fine wines at £25 a bottle. At lunch time there are more snack-type dishes and salads on the menu, plus a reasonably priced dish of the day. Customers may have a starter alone, a main course alone, or a full meal.

Starters
Soup of the Day
Chicken Liver Terrine
Avocado Pear and Prawns
Mushrooms in Garlic
Whitebait

Hot dishes
Spaghetti Bolognaise
Fillet of Pork in Mushroom and Sherry Sauce
Poussin à la Marengo
Lamb Hotpot
Halibut Steak with Cream Sauce
Pork Fillets with Prunes
Steak au Poivre
Vegetables

Sweets
Strawberry Flan
Apple Crumble
Treacle Tart
Ice Cream
Cheese and Biscuits

Planning the menu

The menu is the second half of your showcase but before you indulge all those culinary flights of fancy, take a look at any limiting factors there may be. These will not necessarily cramp your style but they do need to be taken into account and they could point you in quite a different direction.

Space limitations

The most obvious limiting factor is the amount of space you have for the preparation of food. In an existing establishment this will be decided for you, and unless you are planning to make extensive alterations you must work within its confines. If you are converting premises you will have more scope. Do not, however, under-estimate how much space will be required. It is very tempting to cut back the kitchen area in the interests of gaining more revenue but if you cannot supply that larger customer area properly you would have been better off leaving it a little smaller.

When trying to assess how much space you will need, read the section on kitchen equipment on page 132 and remember that additionally, you will need plenty of preparation space. There must also be room for more than one person to work in the kitchen. The actual number will depend on the size of the wine bar, but unless you are only serving snacks, the washing up alone dictates extra help.

If you are stuck with a very small kitchen or no kitchen at all there are various ways of solving the problems. The first is to stick with sandwiches and easy cold plate snacks. This may not sound too exciting to start with but it can work extremely well. At Boos Wine Bar in Marylebone the menu lists a selection of six or seven sandwich fillings, a couple of soups and plates of ham and salad and quiche with home-made cheesecake for dessert. The thing that raises the level of this not very adventurous menu is the quality of the ingredients which are all first class. Judith Rose makes her own soups, quiches and cheesecake and the ham is bought direct from Smithfield and cooked on the bone.

Another city wine bar simply offers cheese sandwiches and smoked salmon together with the proprietor's wife's fruit cake, and the place is packed. Other ideas that have worked well in these circumstances are huge cheese boards, selections of home-made raised pies, jacket baked potatoes with unusual fillings, and home-made toasted sandwiches.

One wine bar owner who was determined not to be defeated by lack of space runs Southeys in Chiswick. This wine bar seats 40. The kitchen is in a partitioned section at the back of the long narrow room, separated from the bar only by a serving counter. Here Mr Southey produces a menu which includes a selection of hot and cold starters, quite a few hot main course dishes, as well as quiches, cold meats and salads. He told me that he prepares and cooks the casseroles for the next day between gaps in the current day's service!

David Belford and his wife who run Coolings in Exeter solved the problem in quite a different way. Despite its size, there is no real kitchen here, and instead of using some of the space to make one they have extended the kitchen in their own home, and all the food is delivered daily to the wine bar. Mr Belford told me that his wife was much happier working in her own environment than she would have been in a dark cellar in the town.

Service methods

Another limiting factor could be the method of service you propose to adopt. Some things are very much easier to offer with table service than they are at a bar counter. Some hot food is difficult to keep warm and still look attractive. On the other hand, a cold buffet can look extemely attractive set out in front of the customer's eyes.

This kind of problem can be solved by serving only those foods which still look attractive even after they have stood on the hot plate for some time. All kinds of pies fall into this category, particularly if they are individual ones. Dishes such as moussaka or those with crunchy or potato toppings also retain their character. Casseroles too can be served along with deep fried foods such as chicken kiev.

Other wine bars display only the cold food and advertise the rest behind the bar, bringing it to the customer's table when it has been dished up in the kitchen. And, of course, some wine bars, particularly the bistro-style ones, offer table service all the time. In some instances the order is taken at the bar, in others at the table. However, it is important to indicate *what* the service is. I have sat patiently in many a wine bar which apparently had waiting staff, sometimes even with those very staff watching me, only to find that I must order at the bar.

Cost limitations

Although quite expensive dishes can sell in rather unlikely areas they are usually part of a mix of dishes which allow a wide range of choice. It is a good idea to go back again to your market research to see what the spending power of the area might be, remembering that very often people will spend more on food for an evening out even though they will not pay a lot for wine. Check out the opposition in terms of eating and see if you can fill a gap in the market.

With the results of this check in mind, think of a range of dishes which will fulfil customer requirements up to the likely price ceiling. Remember that some people will only want a snack but that others could require a full meal. You want to have something on the menu for all likely budget levels. Once you get going you will soon see how the pattern falls.

Value for money remains an important criterion for all the dishes, and it is quite a good idea to offer a dish of the day, particularly at lunch time, at a very reasonable price. Experience will soon show you on what sort of ingredients these should be based. Certainly chicken and pork are consistently the cheapest of the flesh meats and things like liver, eggs and cheese are all pretty economical.

When planning any of your dishes remember that there are quite big seasonal variations in both availability and price and these can work both to your advantage and disadvantage.

Using crops which are in season and which may be particularly cheap for a few weeks because of over-production will help your margins, but it is just as easy to forget that the same foods could get quite expensive at other times of the year so your menus will need to be flexible enough to allow for seasonal changes.

Of course, some foods are available frozen all the

127

year round and many wine bar owners have large regular orders placed with one or other of the frozen food companies. Others pride themselves on always using fresh produce. One wine bar cook told me that despite the extra cost, they had switched from the American Patna style rice to Basmati, the reason being that it can be kept hot for a long time without sticking together and with no deterioration in the flavour. It can sometimes be short-sighted to go for the cheapest ingredients.

The workload

The workload involved in preparing the menu is a very important factor which may not be immediately obvious. Certainly a sandwich or a snack menu will be easier than one with prepared dishes but among the latter there are also big differences.

A hot menu which includes items such as chicken kiev, individual pies, meat or fish *en croûte* and chicken off the bone will take longer to prepare than straightforward casseroles. Grills will be even quicker. A judicious selection of dishes which are easy to prepare, with a few more elaborate ones mixed in to impress discerning customers, may be the answer.

Even with cold food and salads there will be differences in the workload involved with each dish. If you are not sure of preparation times it is worth keeping a record in the early days, and if a particular dish is very time-consuming, take it off the menu. Of course, if it has gained a following in the meantime you will be stuck with it!

The choice of menu must also depend upon the skill of your cook. It is a mistake to put an elaborate dish or a fancy sauce on the menu if your cook is simply not up to producing it. Very often you or your partner will be doing the cooking and if you have not had previous experience of cooking in bulk you could make life very hard for yourself. Some dishes lend themselves to large-scale catering much more easily than others. It is probably a good idea to try out some of the recipes you are planning to use on a buffet party or two at home.

The guiding rule should be to offer only that which you know you can really do well. It is far better to offer a smaller menu which you are sure of than a larger one which may or may not be up to standard.

Popular dishes and specialities
There are fashions in food just as there are in clothing and cosmetics and it is worth studying current trends. Most people like to see a menu which is adventurous or which looks interesting. On the other hand, as with wine, they tend to stick to the familiar. The sight of beef bourguignonne or coq au vin on a menu is reassuring. They have had it before and know what it tastes like. In time they may also come to try the other items on your menu.

During your initial research into wine bars and what they have to offer, make a note of the menus and then, when you have a reasonable number, compare them. You will find that there are certain dishes or types of dishes which come up every time and you should at least consider including them on your own menu. You can, after all, make your own versions of them.

This is not to say that you cannot set a fashion of your own. If you have some specialities which you are really good at making, the chances are that they will catch on. These specialities might even form the basis of all the food in the bar. However, you must still try to cater for all tastes. Pam Diamond of Tempters tries always to include one each of the following types: a spicy dish, a cream-based dish, a fruity dish, and a very straight-forward homely dish. Everything is served with rice, so she does not have to worry about vegetables.

In the wine bars I have visited were menus based on French provincial cooking, Italian pasta, traditional English cooking, international or mixed dishes and even a vegetarian menu in Edinburgh. Of these, British-based cookery was probably the most prevalent with some excellent food on offer. Game is usually a speciality here, but haggis, Scottish beef, Aylesbury duck and local free-range chicken all turn up quite frequently.

The Pipe of Port in Southend specialises in this type of food so I was rather surprised to see frogs' legs on the menu. Apparently they were extremely popular and some of the customers came just for them! So do not be afraid of inserting an inconsistent note if you think it will work.

Some of the more unusual ideas I have come across include barbecued spare ribs with jacket potatoes, fisherman's platter – hot with a mixture of deep fried fish and shellfish and cold with a mixture of smoked and pickled fish with various sauces – delicate vegetable terrines with beautiful patterns running through them, chicken breasts with fresh limes, salmon trout *en croûte* and home-made ice creams, including a coçktail ice cream.

However, nearly all the wine bars offering these choices also offered a plain grilled steak. As Pam Diamond put it, 'There is always one in a party who will only eat plain food and if he does not get it none of the party will come back again.'

If you have decided which wines you will be specialising in, then obviously it would make sense to carry the German theme through in the food if you have chosen German wines as a speciality. This idea can also work if the bar itself has a special theme. Sometimes there will be dishes which will be particularly appropriate to it, but even if there are not you can use the theme to give interesting names to your dishes.

Changing the menu

Thinking up one menu is simply not enough. You may find that the evening trade is quite different from your lunch-time trade and this could necessitate two menus or at least an expanded, or contracted one for the evening.

If you are successful you will build up a reservoir of regular customers and they will not want to see the same menu every time they come. Some wine bars have to change the menu daily. One inner city wine bar owner told me that most of his customers come in two or three times a week. To cope with this he offers a range of four dishes which are changed every day. This is backed up with a basic repertoire of a couple of dozen firm favourites which do not change very much. Sometimes one of the daily offerings becomes so popular it joins the regular menu.

In other wine bars the menu is changed weekly or changes are made as certain dishes run out and new ones are introduced.

Buying the food

Bulk buying naturally springs to mind when the subject of catering comes up, but unless your wine bar can seat quite a large number, you may find that the size of your order does not really rate a wholesale account.

There are, of course, numerous cash and carry outlets, some of which, if used sensibly, can save you money. But if possible, check them out first. Some offer only very small discounts and the quality may leave something to be desired. The right cash and carry is very useful for groceries and hardware materials but less useful for fresh meat, fruit and vegetables. If you are planning to buy frozen food in any quantity you may get a better deal direct from the manufacturers, many of whom are geared up to deliver to the catering trade.

If you have a local market, astute buying here could keep costs right down. It will also be easier to take advantage of summer gluts and to make a feature of local produce on the menu. Otherwise you might come to an arrangement with local retail suppliers for discounts on large orders. Such arrangements are often the best. The local supplier gets to know you and your business and the personal contact can be very valuable.

Cooking methods and equipment

Leaving aside the few wine bars which buy in most

of their food there are two schools of thought in the trade. The first is the 'fresh every day' brigade. In these wine bars the food has been freshly cooked on the premises that morning and many of the ingredients too will be fresh that day.

Gales wine bar in Llangollen is one of these. Richard Gale is convinced that a small menu of superb quality is preferable to a large choice. His menu features one hot dish only, though this is different each day. In addition there are usually one or two hot soups and a small selection of cold dishes and salads. These too change frequently. Richard told me that his cooks now have a repertoire of over 100 soups, all of which are costed. The only exception to the 'fresh every day' rule is the home-made ice cream and this is so popular that it almost falls into this category. This method of operation does have advantages of scale and there are fewer problems of wastage.

The second school is heavily dependent upon the freezer. Dishes are batch-baked in advance and withdrawn from storage as and when they are needed. Very often wine bars using this method also include freshly cooked dishes on the day's menus. None of the successful owners operating this type of catering gets complaints from the customers, quite the contrary, but they do admit that great care has to be exercised in choosing dishes which will be completely unaffected by their sojourn in the freezer.

Careful control must be exercised over packaging and the quantities which are frozen together. The method also involves greater investment in equipment for freezing not only in freezers but also in microwave ovens.

Equipment

However you are planning to organise the production of your food, you will inevitably need a fair amount of equipment. Staff in the kitchen can be expensive, so quite apart from basic equipment, you will need to think about labour saving gadgets such as processors and mixers. Here is a run-down of the major categories of equipment you should consider together with some points to note. This list does not take into account any equipment which might be needed to fulfil the requirements of the Food Hygiene Regulations discussed in Chapter 4.

Cookers
The choice of gas or electricity may be dictated by the availability of gas mains in the vicinity. However, modern electric cookers are almost as quickly adjustable as gas. If you are buying second-hand, I would recommend gas if at all possible.

The size and number of the cookers will be determined by the number you expect to cater for. But double ovens are useful, and fan-assisted ovens mean slightly faster cooking and an even temperature throughout. Separately built-in hobs and ovens could also help if space is restricted.

Microwave cookers
These are probably vital if you plan to freeze any quantity of food. There are very many versions on the market but the commercial models, though more expensive than their domestic counterparts, are much more efficient.

Freezers
The choice between chest and upright freezers might be decided by space restrictions. However, if the freezer is likely to be in constant use, chest freezers take in less heat. On the other hand, it is easier to find things in an upright freezer.

Fridges and chilling units
Here again the size and number will depend upon the size of your operation. Remember that if you are freezing a lot of food the quicker it is chilled the better and safer it will be. A special fridge or chilling unit for this purpose could be a good investment. Food left to cool in a warm kitchen could be dangerous.

Fryers, infra-red grills and toasters
Depending on the kind of food you plan to serve, there is a mass of specialist equipment to help you. An electric deep-fat fryer is wonderful for chips and it also means that you can startle the customers with one or two deep-fried specialities.

Peelers, mixers, food processors and mincers
One or two of these will probably find a place in the kitchen. Make sure you buy the heavy-duty versions if you go for the domestic makes. The choice between a mixer and a food processor will depend on the sort of cooking you are doing. The processor is a very useful maid-of-all work, good with vegetables and meat as well as with soups and purées. The mixer, on the other hand, is the baker's friend.

Miscellaneous electrical equipment
Depending on the other equipment you decide to buy, you may want to consider electric whisks, toasters, kettles, carving knives or slicers.

All these items represent a considerable expenditure and some of them can be very expensive indeed. One answer is to buy some of them second-hand. This may mean a less convenient appliance in the short term, but as the business starts to make money some of it can be ploughed back into the business in the form of new equipment.

Another solution is to hire the expensive items. The advantage of this is that you do not have too much money tied up in unrealistic assets. Hiring can also help you to make up your mind whether or not you really need the item in question. If you do, you can always invest in your own equipment and return the hired item. Always make sure that your equipment is well maintained. Failure to do so could invalidate your insurance. A not inconsiderable investment will also have to be made in basic kitchen equipment and utensils. Unless your wine bar is very small, your existing stock of domestic equipment is likely to be inadequate. Even large household pans will not cook vegetables for more than eight or ten. This area of expenditure also needs to be borne in mind when menu planning. Individual pies, for example, are very attractive but may necessitate buying a quantity of the right size dish.

Here's a checklist to start you off. Remember to add to it any specialist items appropriate to your menus such as raised pie moulds, butter curlers, ice cream scoops or egg slicers.

Kitchen crockery and utensils
Large scale measuring equipment
Large vegetable and stew pans
Large frying pans
Fish kettle and steamers
Large casseroles
Roasting tins
Baking trays and tins
A good selection of chef's kitchen knives
Mixing bowls and basins
Grating and squeezing equipment
Chopping boards
Rolling pin, cutters and dredgers
Heavy-duty can opener
Colanders and strainers
Timers and cook's thermometer
Melon and potato baller, julienne cutters etc
Piping equipment
Moulds and pâté dishes
Plates, bowls and dishes for displaying the food

Presenting the food

The chances are that at least some of your food will be on display at the counter, but important though the look of this is, the first notice of your food must come from the menu displayed at the door in printed form or on chalkboards. Chalkboards at this point have the advantage of attracting attention but you could get into trouble with the local authority if they are obstructing the pavement in any way.

Inside the wine bar chalkboards are again the most popular form of presenting the day's menu. They are, of course, totally flexible and not only can changes be incorporated every day without the menu looking a mess, but dishes which have run out can be erased immediately and there will be fewer disappointed customers. However, some wine bars do have handwritten menus which look most attractive.

Explanations of some of the more unfamiliar dishes, particularly if you are introducing them for the first time or have invented them yourself, are a useful guide for the customer and can encourage people to try things which they might have passed by. Short notes can also allay surprises which might or might not be pleasurable. Garlic mushrooms which I encountered in Chiswick turned out not to be a cold hors d'oeuvre but a hot dish very similar to snails in garlic butter. It was very good but not at all what I had expected. In another bar the relatively expensive plate of smoked salmon had obviously come out of a frozen pack and had not even been trimmed. In fact a very disappointing buy which did not line up with its promise on the menu. Any counter display must be its own advertisement and it is important to keep plates and bowls topped up. Three-quarters empty dishes do not look very attractive. Some items dry out if they are left standing for too long, so small batches should be prepared. Hot food has its own problems and I believe it is usually better left undisplayed.

Very often a good impression can be implanted by some of the smaller touches of food presentation. For example, is it possible to serve the bread warm, can you make sure that the garnishes are not wilting, can you dispense with pre-packed items such as butter and sugar?

A little thought around the edges of your menu should lead you to some goodwill builders. I was impressed by the attractively large salad bowls used in one wine bar. Of course, they were not filled to the top but they did look attractive. In another olives garnishing the taramasalata were lusciously plump and studded with chopped garlic, and in a third, a choice of Indian or China tea was on offer for customers who did not like coffee.

Coffee

This brings us to another very useful profit centre. Sales of coffee in wine bars can be very high indeed. The Archduke Wine Bar, built underneath the arches at Waterloo Station, sells over 2500 cups of coffee per week. It is, of course, a very large bar but smaller ones can still expect to sell between 1000 and 1500 cups per week, particularly if shoppers are encouraged to come in for a coffee out of licensing hours.

Good coffee goes with good wine and wine bar customers can be very discerning coffee drinkers so it pays to choose the best. If you are not sure what the demand will be, start with single cup filter coffees. They may seem expensive to buy but you can still make at least 15p to 20p on them. If the demand starts to exceed a dozen or more cups an hour you will need to reconsider this.

Single cup filter coffee is certainly the simplest way to make coffee. The pre-measured quantity is placed on top of the cup and the boiling water is poured into the filter. There is nothing to go wrong and there is no outlay on expensive equipment – all you need is a kettle.

However, if demand is high it may be just as quick and easy to use one of the many coffee making machines which are on the market. Talk to one or two specialist suppliers such as Kenco or the Nairobi Coffee and Tea Company. They will give you personal advice tailored to the needs of your particular situation. They will advise on both the types of coffee to serve and the machines to use. It may be that you will want to offer two or three different kinds of coffee or perhaps a lighter coffee by day and a darker, stronger version in the evenings.

Once the system has been installed the main point to watch is that the coffee is always reasonably fresh. Never try to make more than you will need in one hour and never allow the coffee or milk to boil. Always use fresh coffee in the correct measures and allow sufficient time for infusion.

If you have a full licence and are serving full meals or are specialising in the bistro type of wine bar you might find that there is a demand for liqueur coffee. A wine bar in the north makes a big feature of its liqueur coffees, offering six or seven using Irish and Scotch whisky, Tia Maria and some fruit-based brandies.

Pricing the food

The same sort of pricing criteria for wines outlined in Chapter 7 hold good for your food. However, working out the cost of the food itself is a more time-consuming operation. Each dish needs to be costed out separately.

Make a list of all the ingredients in a particular recipe and make a note of the number the batch is expected to serve. Remember to include items like salt and pepper, herbs and spices and small amounts of cooking oil or flour. These items are easy to disregard but they need to be replaced quite regularly. Make a note of the cost against each ingredient. The total will give you the basic cost of the dish. Now you will need to add on a percentage of the fuel costs and all the other overheads which have to be paid for.

Every so often you should check the actual basic costs of producing a particular dish against the above estimate to see if you have got the calculation right. This exercise will also tell you if prices are rising and whether there are any seasonal variations which significantly affect the cost of the dish.

Unfortunately, with food, this is not the end of the calculations. Unlike wine, food cannot just be returned to the storage unit if it does not sell. You must therefore include an allowance for wastage. This will be pure guess-work to start with but once a particular dish has been offered to the customers for a period of time you will be able to work out the average number of portions which are likely to be taken up. You will then not only be in a better position to decide exactly how much to make but also able to cost in a figure for wastage. From that calculation you can work out a percentage profit per portion.

This is a particularly useful exercise for expensive items of food which might prove tempting to the staff. If the profit levels start to fall below 80 per cent the chances are that there is something wrong. If you do suspect that this is happening you can institute a stringent portion control policy by quite simply counting out every portion yourself and making sure that every single one is accounted for.

Clearing away

Unfortunately, the catering job does not stop once the customer has wined and dined; there is the clearing up to do and this requires just as much care and organisation as the more interesting job of preparing the food.

The first problem is the washing up and this can be quite substantial even in a fairly small wine bar. Part-time helpers are one answer but some sort of specialised equipment will help to stop the wages bill rising too far and can be rather more hygienic. You do not necessarily need electrical equipment, though this is very good. There are, for example, twin-tub glass washers which, though not mechanical, do have constantly changing water. This sort of equipment may, indeed, be recommended by the public health authorities. Remember that frequent washing up, by whatever method, will also mean breakages and they should be allowed for in your calculations for variable costs.

The second problem is disposing of the waste and the Food Hygiene Regulations lay down some stringent requirements. The first step is to make sure that waste food is never allowed to accumulate in the kitchen. Staff should be encouraged to work as tidily as possible and to clear rubbish into the waste bin after each step in the preparation of food. Waste food from the wine bar should also go straight into the bin.

The next step is to ensure that kitchen bins are emptied as soon as they are full or at the end of each cooking session. The bins should be washed and disinfected equally regularly. Alternatively, you can use disposable wet-resistant paper or plastic refuse bags. Units for the latter may be free standing, attached to walls or inside cupboard doors.

Outside the premises you should have a purpose-built area for bins with a raised base and a nearby water supply for regular sluicing down. The bins should have tight-fitting lids and should not be filled to overflowing as they will thus obviously attract vermin.

Another way of disposing of kitchen rubbish is through a waste disposal unit flushing it down the sink. Most modern equipment grinds the rubbish so finely that there is no risk of clogging the drains – a point likely to be checked by the Public Health Officer – and with safety devices to stop it eating up your cutlery.

Chapter 9
Staffing

It has often been said that a businessman's troubles begin when he starts to employ other people, and with 16 or more extensive Acts of Parliament covering the subject there could be some justice in the remark. However, unless your wine bar is very small indeed you will need help. Even the tiny Boos Wine Bar employs one part-time helper though Judith and Michael Rose do as much as they can themselves.

Part-time staff are an attractive proposition for many wine bars and quite a few operate with a husband and wife team working more than full time plus as many as six or seven part-time helpers. Larger wine bars like Coolings in Exeter employ mainly full-time staff with only a few part-timers. In contrast, the Pipe of Port in Southend employs more part-time than full-time staff but there are four full-time partners employed in the business.

Sometimes the choice of full- or part-time staff is dictated by the local labour conditions. A wine bar owner in the south west told me that he had the greatest difficulty in finding the right sort of staff and when he did their hours were fixed more to suit their needs than his. 'It's the only way to keep them,' he commented.

The difficulty of finding the right staff is a recurring refrain in most parts of the country. Wine bars are not always attractive or convenient to the local labour force and evening jobs can be particularly hard to fill. Nor do you really want to employ just anybody. A good wine bar waiter or waitress should ideally know something about the wines, have a pleasant and friendly personality and also be a good sales person.

Choosing staff

Whatever the state of the local job market, it is very important to make the right decisions in picking people to work for you, and if you are not very careful it can be a bit of a gamble. The first step is to ask yourself exactly what you need staff for. The sort of areas in which you might want to employ people include serving the customers, either at the bar or at the table, preparing and cooking the food, cleaning the premises and washing up and possibly general heavy work around the bar. How many people will you need in each area and how much can you do yourself?

The next question is how much can you afford to pay in wages and how can this amount best be apportioned between the jobs which need to be done? Add to this a list of the sort of personality traits which are important in wine bar work and you will have the basis of a good series of job descriptions.

Very often one of the partners in a wine bar venture will do the cooking. However, this may not be practicable or this partner may not want to continue in the role of cook after the business has got off the ground. The problem then is to find someone who is an equally good cook or competent enough to carry out existing recipes with care and attention to detail, and who can withstand the pressures of working in a wine bar kitchen. Despite the high quality of the food in most wine bars, very few of them use trained chefs and quite a number of owners specifically make the point that a good amateur cook produces exactly the sort of food the customer likes. However, I have come across one sort of half-way house situation where students from the local catering college were employed to very good effect as part-time cooks.

Interviewing

Once you have got all your job descriptions together you will be in a much better position to draft an advertisement. The job description should also form the basis for the contract of employment and for the criteria to be used at interviews.

The interview is very important because it gives you a chance to measure the various applicants against your job description. Make a list of questions to ask and make sure that they are framed in such a way that you do not just get 'yes' and 'no' answers. Remember, too, that the applicant will want to know full details of the position you are offering. Anticipate the interviewee's own questions and have the answers ready. Here's a list of the points you should check when interviewing for bar or waiting staff.

Checklist of assessment at the interview
1. How competent are the interviewees at the job you have in mind? What is their previous experience?
2. What is their track record like? Have they had any previous jobs?
3. Are their personalities likely to appeal to customers and will they be able to deal politely with difficult situations?
4. Do they know anything at all about wine?
5. Do you think they will make good sales people?
6. Do you have any reason to think that they might not be honest?
7. Have you asked for and taken up references? These are best taken up by telephone as most employers are prepared to talk more freely if there is no written record.

Contract of employment

Having decided whom you want to employ the next step is to issue a contract of employment. This must be issued to all employees who are going to work for you for more than 16 hours a week. It should be a straightforward document which covers the terms of employment. It must cover the following points:

1. The job title.
2. The rate of pay and how it is calculated.
3. How frequently the money is to be paid.
4. The normal working hours and the terms and conditions relating to them.
5. Holidays and holiday pay.
6. Provision for sick pay.
7. Pension and pension schemes.
8. Notice required by both parties.
9. Any disciplinary rules relating to the job.
10. Grievance procedures.

The Department of Employment issues a leaflet 'Written statement of main terms and conditions of employment' which covers the subject in more detail. Copies can be obtained from a Social Security Office or local Jobcentre.

Working with staff

Once you have taken on staff there is a whole host of regulations which must be observed. Some of them are concerned with the employee's working conditions and you should familiarise yourself with the following:

Shops Act 1950. Section 21 of this Act contains special provisions relating to assistants employed in premises for the sale of refreshments. The Offices, Shops and Railway Premises Act 1963 is also relevant here.

Health and Safety at Work Act 1974. These regulations are very extensive so check with your local Health and Safety Executive Office. Local authorities enforce some parts of the Act, and government and other central bodies other parts. The Health and Safety Commission publish some useful literature including 'The 1974 Act outlined, advice to employers', and 'Reporting on accidents'. Another useful source of information is the Royal Society for the Prevention of Accidents.

Sex Discrimination Act, Equal Pay Act, and the Race Relations Act. The requirements of these Acts need to be borne in mind when advertising for staff and in their subsequent treatment.

Training

Once you have taken on staff you must make sure that they are perfectly clear about what they are expected to do. A few hurried instructions on the first day really are not good enough and you will need to spend some time with each new member of staff explaining exactly what you are trying to achieve in your wine bar. Encourage the bar and waiting staff to take a greater interest in wine generally and make sure that they know the background to the wines which are on your list. The more you can interest your staff in the job in hand the better they are likely to carry it out.

You should also make sure that the staff understand your attitude to customers. Difficult customers will need need to be handled carefully and it is a good idea to work out a procedure in advance for dealing with the more awkward occurrences. Make sure that your staff call you on to the scene at once. It is much easier to support your staff if they have not already been provoked into a display of temper. It is also easier for you, as owner, to take any major criticisms. Indeed, you should want to hear them. All the complaints may not be valid but some of them could point the way to useful improvements.

The whole question of your relationship with your staff is important, not only for the harmonious running of the wine bar but also in terms of building up personal loyalty. There will be times when you will need your staff to put in extra time or to help out with jobs which are not normally theirs. Remember that the relationship is not one sided and you must also work at it.

Staff honesty

A loyal staff is also more likely to be an honest

staff. This is always an emotive area and most people tend to think that because a person seems to have an honest and open personality that they *are* honest. The truth of the matter is that you simply cannot tell by looking at someone whether they are honest or not. Indeed, as some owners have found to their cost, you still cannot be sure even after a year or more of working together.

The only way to be reasonably confident is to keep temptation to an absolute minimum. Free food and a glass of wine at meal times or at closing time 'legalise' pilfering which is almost sure to take place otherwise. Install stock control systems for both food and wine and indeed anything else which is sold in the bar. Try to make these systems simple to operate and difficult to cheat. Lastly, and perhaps most importantly, handle as much of the money as you can yourself. You might also think about taking out fidelity guarantees.

Sadly, the statistics show that the staff of a catering establishment are the largest single cause of loss, and this loss is not only in terms of money but in terms of reputation. A bad staff will give bad service. Dissatisfied customers will not often complain. They simply do not come again, and worse, they tell their friends not to come either.

Some owners have felt that the need for part-time staff could be more safely filled by working with friends. Unfortunately, this does not usually provide the answer. However much you trust your friends, the truth of the matter is that they are just as susceptible to temptation as anyone else. They may also find that they do not like taking orders from you. As one owner put it, 'It is much safer to make friends of your staff than to make staff of your friends.'

Fidelity guarantee
This is insurance taken out by the employer naming the member or members of staff who have access to the takings and the stock, and it covers him in case of theft. It is underwritten by an insurance company who probably check up on the

people concerned to see that they do not have criminal records or anything known to their detriment.

Getting rid of staff

The various Employment Acts lay down very specific criteria for both firing staff and redundancy. Here again the provisions are intricate. Booklets on the subject include:

'Unfairly dismissed?'
'Rights on termination of employment'
'The law on unfair dismissal – guidance for small firms'
'Procedures for handling redundancies'
'Suspension on medical grounds under Health and Safety Regulations'
'Rules governing continuous employment and a week's pay'

Obtain copies of these publications from Jobcentres or the Advisory, Conciliation and Arbitration Service (ACAS).

Many people view the legislation as being totally unfair to the employer. This is not really the case. For example, the qualifying period for alleged unfair dismissal claims was extended in the 1980 legislation to one year for most small businesses and to two years if you employ fewer than 20 people. If you have kept someone for this length of time without sorting things out with them, it is only right that they should be protected. Even if your staff have not been with you for two years you must still give one week's notice, or payment in lieu, unless the employee has been with you for less than four weeks.

A point to watch when buying a going concern is that you might have a problem if you buy a wine bar lock, stock and barrel, together with staff. You may not like or trust some of the staff or you may be organising things on a different basis and thus need fewer staff with the result that the staff will be made redundant. Despite the fact that you did not hire these people you are stuck with your responsibility as their current employer.

Employment records

If you employ staff you will be responsible for deducting PAYE from their wages and for fulfilling the provisions of the Social Securities Acts.

PAYE has to be paid monthly to the Inland Revenue. You will receive from the tax office a tax deduction card for each employee. Remember that if you are operating as a limited company you will have to fill in a card for yourself and your co-director(s); this must be done even if you employ no one else at all.

The tax deduction card has space for weekly or monthly entries and the details required include details of tax, pay for each period and for the year to date. Your local Inland Revenue office will also supply you with tax tables and the employees' tax code so that you can read off the appropriate figures.

An itemised statement must also be produced for each employee on or before each pay day. This must show gross wages, net wages, deductions and the reasons for them, and details of part payments such as special overtime rates.

At the end of the tax year (5 April) you will have to fill in two further forms: P60, which goes to each individual employee, and P35, which is a summary for the Inland Revenue. Form P45 is filled in when an employee leaves.

For more information, obtain the following booklets from the Inland Revenue or Jobcentres:

'Employer's guide to PAYE'
'Itemised pay statements'

National Insurance contributions are collected at the same time as PAYE. Contact your local Department of Health and Social Security Office or your local Social Security Office for more advice and look out for the following leaflets:

NP 15 'Employer's guide to National Insurance contributions'
NI 208 'National Insurance contribution rates'

Employment legislation

Here is a checklist of the legislation dealing with employment. Copies of the various Acts can usually be obtained from HMSO.

Accidents and Dangerous Occurrences Regulations 1979

Children and Young Persons Act 1983

Employers Liability (Compulsory Insurance) Act 1969

Employment Acts 1980 and 1982

The Employment Protection (Consolidation) Act 1978

Equal Pay Act 1970

Fair Wages Resolution 1946

Food Hygiene (General) Regulations 1970

Health and Safety at Work Act 1974

Information for Employees Regulations 1965

Offices, Shops and Railway Premises Act 1963

Race Relations Act 1976

Rehabilitation of Offenders Act 1974

Sex Discrimination Act 1975

Shops Act 1950

Social Securities (Claims and Payment) Regulations 1979

Social Security Act 1975

Social Security Pensions Act 1975

Unfair Contract Terms Act 1977

Chapter 10

Keeping the Wine Bar Full

It is not enough to get the wine bar going – you have got to keep it full. Novelty value may bring the customers in to start with and a good wine list and menu plus friendly service will keep them there – but only for a while. It is fatal to sit back and think, 'Well, I have got it right now.' You must keep people interested. If you do not, you may be in for a nasty surprise at the speed with which customers can disappear.

You will certainly get plenty of well meaning advice about how you may improve the bar and some of it could be quite useful. So listen and be tolerant but do make your own decisions.

Stimulating interest

The first step in keeping customers' interest is to make sure that they are aware of all the different types of wine on your list and the dishes on your menu. The sort of promotional activity outlined on pages 115-16 in Chapter 7 should help to encourage your customers to be more adventurous. This is important in itself because you will do far better with customers who are tempted into trying a variety of dishes and wines than with a bar full of people having the dish of the day and a glass of the house wine.

But 'wine of the month' promotions and the like are not enough in themselves. You must also introduce new wines and new dishes. Quite often these introductions serve not only as a talking point and interest-arouser but also as a pointer to future favourites.

The menu at Coolings in Exeter features quite a

high proportion of vegetarian dishes because the proprietor ran a vegetarian week fairly early on in his operation there. The dishes proved to be so popular that he retained most of them on his regular menu.

The same sort of thing can also happen with wines. David Belford negotiated a special price deal on Lambrusco and featured it as a 'wine by the glass' special offer. It became so popular that it is now among the top sellers of all his wines.

However, new introductions need to be carefully balanced against the existing list and menus. Too many new introductions will offend the conservative approach of many customers. Nor should you buy in too much of any novelty item. It may sell well, but it could fail. The Lambrusco did well at Coolings and items such as English wines, Tyrol wines, game specialities, cold smoked lamb and local cheeses have succeeded elsewhere. But those same English wines have fallen flat in other bars, so take as much care with your new introductions as you did with the initial list and menu and always remember to keep your customer profile in mind.

It is sometimes more difficult to persuade customers to try new items on the menu than it is to get them to sample a different glass of wine. At Tempters, Pam and Allan Diamond tempt their customers with small morsels of their new dishes and will rush into the kitchen for a sample the moment the customer shows any interest.

Small touches here and there also help to boost the wine bar's image. At Boos in Marylebone the customers are offered small bowls of dry biscuits, and in other wine bars this sort of tiny snack is extended to include salted nuts, crisps and olives. One very enterprising wine bar owner in Sussex offers customers two or three tiny titbits or canapés on a little tray and these come with every order between 5.30 and 7.30 pm.

Novelty drinks vary from straightforward wine-based drinks such as kir and buck's fizz to exotic and complicated cocktails. The latter are very much a fashion of the early eighties and it could be that their popularity will not last. However, while they are in fashion they could be an extra source of profit. Of course, to serve them, you must have a full licence.

Another service to the customer and profit centre for the wine bar owner is cigars. In the right location the offer of a good cigar presented in a humidifier at the coffee stage can add a useful percentage to the bill. Cigars have to be kept at a suitable humidity but many of the importers will supply wooden humidifiers, sometimes with your bar's name on the top.

Coffee, covered in some detail on pages 137-8, can be another business draw. Quite a few bars which are situated in busy shopping or commercial centres operate an open-all-day policy, offering coffee and croissants at breakfast time, coffee and biscuits or cakes mid-morning and mid-afternoon as well as serving coffee after meals. The Pipe of Port in Southend also offers sandwiches on Saturday mornings and these are very popular with local shoppers.

Take advantage of the seasons too, if you can. Tables and chairs in the garden or patio or even on the pavement are always popular in good weather. However, you had better check with the local council that the chairs and tables on the pavement will not be considered an obstruction. In winter an open log fire or even a simulated one is a very welcoming gesture.

Flexibility is one of the key notes in keeping a wine bar full. You must change with the times. One Midlands wine bar owner told me that he had had to trade down quite considerably over the last two or three years: the changing industrial situation had not only put people out of work but had severely curtailed 'expenses' entertaining. In other areas where new light and service industries are developing the scene is quite different. Young executives are moving in and though they do not have money to fling around they can afford the middle range wine and a steak or two.

'Happy hour'

Views on whether or not to institute a 'happy hour', offering reduced-price drinks, are divided. There are those who say quite categorically that you should be able to make the business work without having to give food or drink away. As one owner put it, 'I want my customers to come for the atmosphere and the enjoyment, not to get tanked up at a cheap rate.'

There are, however, other owners who believe that their 'happy hour' brings in customers who might otherwise have gone elsewhere and some of them stay on for the rest of the evening. Others come back for an evening out at a later date. Bottle-screw Bill's, the Davy wine bar in Exeter, operates a 'champagne happy hour' between 12 noon and 1 pm, and 7 to 8 pm, and the manager told me that they sell quite a lot of champagne they would not sell otherwise. The 'happy hour' offer reduces the price of champagne by £2 and thus brings it down to the level of a good claret or Burgundy.

Private functions

A wine bar can be a great place for a party and, provided that you do not lose other customers because of it, a party is good for a wine bar. Private function rooms are very useful but this could detract from the wine bar atmosphere. Much better is a partially screened section of the wine bar which can be separated off for the party. At Bubbles in Mayfair there is a raised section at the back of the bar which is often hired for private functions.

Indeed, it is probably worth actively encouraging this type of use. Depending on your location you may be looking for business at lunch time or in the evening and both these times are suitable for office celebrations, retirements and leaving parties. Make sure that your business customers know of the facility and try circularising the personnel departments of the businesses in your area giving details of the space you have to offer and any special terms you can give. However, businesses are not necessarily speedy payers, so you may wish to consider asking for a deposit in advance and the balance on the day. Clubs and societies without premises of their own or which are looking for a more exciting environment for anniversary or Christmas parties offer another opportunity. Have a look in the Yellow Pages of your telephone directory or on the library notice boards to find secretaries' names and addresses. Town hall information deparments often hold such lists.

Birthday and anniversary parties for private individuals are another possibility. One bar I came across specialised in offering suitable cakes and gateaux for these parties, another featured christening teas, and yet another wedding breakfasts – mornings only!

Special events

Another way of keeping up interest in your wine bar is to offer special events from time to time. Some of these must logically fall on or around the day concerned such as Hallowe'en, Christmas, Twelfth Night, Valentine's Day, May Day and Midsummer Day celebrations. Others can be geared to boosting business at quiet times.

Nigel Ravenshill of Wheels recommends keeping a diary of bookings throughout the year. This, together with a look at your sales records, will tell you when the bad patches were in the previous year. In this way you will get to know the pattern of your trade and will be able to turn your promotional activities to best advantage.

Here again, you must ask yourself the question, 'What will my customers enjoy and how much will they be prepared to pay for it?' Very often a promotion of this kind involves a special meal and it is easy to price this beyond the average customer's pocket simply because you want to do something different. If at all possible keep the price of special meals within sight of the average amount spent in your bar.

Ideas for events include the following, but no doubt you will be able to think up many more.

Summer barbecues
Beaujolais nouveau promotions and meals
French, Italian, German evenings
Wine tastings from specific regions
Country and western evenings

You may be able to tie your promotional evening to a local event such as well-dressing, cheese rolling or a yearly market. Wine bars near race courses could offer post-racing dinners and those near to historical buildings or monuments could use the local history to build up a suitable theme.

There are one or two points to watch with both private functions and your own events. It may be that you will want an extension to the normal licensing hours. Special application can be made to the magistrates' court for extensions to the licence for particular days. However, you will have to give full details of the event and show why an extension is necessary. If the extension is granted you should inform the police that you have a certificate to open longer than usual on the day in question.

Live music can be an attraction in a wine bar but it needs careful handling. First you must apply for an entertainment licence. This licence is granted by the local council and may be valid for a year or for such shorter period as may be specified. The information called for by the council varies from one authority to another but you will usually be required to give notice of your application to the Chief Officer of Police and the fire authority as well as the council. Some councils will also want to see the plans of your premises before any application can be made, so check out the details well in advance.

Second, it is no good expecting the introduction of any old live performer to magically boost a slack Monday evening. You must choose a type of music which will appeal to your customers and then test it out. Start with one of your better evenings when you have a good crowd in and the artist can be seen performing at his best. When you are sure that the artist is the right one for your bar and word of the new attraction spreads, you can then introduce your artist on a second night, hopefully with equally profitable results.

Publicity and public relations

In a sense all the activities outlined in this chapter so far are forms of public relations. But if you are going to offer special attractions you will want as many people as possible to know about them and this probably means advertising beyond the confines of your own premises.

The very first need for publicity comes when you open the wine bar. You will want your entire catchment area to know that you are there. In a small town this may simply mean advertising the actual opening date, for as the owner of a wine bar in a small country town told me, 'Everyone knew that there was to be a new wine bar almost before we had signed the lease and gained the licence.' In a big town or city the grapevine does not operate in quite the same way and you will need to advertise your presence.

There are various ways of doing this. The first is paid advertising in newspapers, magazines and local radio and you might even consider a small advertisement in the local Yellow Pages, entertainment guides or student handbooks.

Local newspapers offer fairly reasonable advertising rates but remember that the lower the rate the lower the circulation. There may be more than one daily paper in your area and it will be worth checking their catchment areas to see if they correspond with yours and if there are any differences between the areas in which they are popular. You should also consider the relative merits of the weekly newspapers in the area. These may not be read to the same extent but if your announcement is on the entertainments page near the cinema and club advertising, it is more likely to be seen and it will stay in the house for a full week compared with one day for an advertisement in a daily paper.

Local magazines also offer the same advantages of a longer home life and this means that over the period your advertisement may be seen by a number of people. County magazines are well worth considering as they concentrate on social and leisure activities and are usually taken by those who have a little extra money to spend. Entertainment guides may be even nearer to your target market particularly in tourist areas where you may expect a percentage of transient trade. Indeed, if this is a feature of the area in which you are located, you may want to consider taking some form of advertising in the local hotels' information packs for guests.

Quite a few wine bar owners I have interviewed had tried local newspaper advertising around the time that they opened but most had mixed feelings on the subject. They all felt that it was difficult to tell how many of the people who visited the bar in the first few weeks came as a result of the advertising or of straightforward curiosity.

Local radio is another possibility and Steve Jones of the Pipe of Port made his local radio advertising pay off by using a very original approach. He chose a spot around 11.30 on Friday and Saturday evenings when he reckoned everyone who had been out would be driving home. These people were a prime target in that they were probably people who went out regularly. He used a very soft sell approach simply wishing listeners a safe drive home and suggesting that maybe they would like to try the Pipe of Port next week. The advertisements certainly did the job of getting the wine bar known.

Another equally successful approach was used by a new inner city wine bar. Attractive handbills were printed, not so large that they would take up too much space, but large enough to be eye-catching, and the owner persuaded a good percentage of the office blocks in the area to post them on their staff notice boards. The result was an influx of both business entertaining and office lunches.

Some wine bar owners have offered opening discounts or have had a party to launch the bar. However, most of them felt that this had been rather a waste of money and on closer inspection it was mainly found to be because they had invited the wrong people. By and large, the only people it is really worth entertaining to more than a complimentary drink are the so-called 'opinion formers'. Obviously the media belong to this category and it is well worth inviting representatives of the newspapers and radio stations in the area. If you are lucky they may do a feature on your bar, and even if they do not go this far, you have increased your chances of being included in any general article on eating out in the area.

Other opinion formers may be local hoteliers and the tourist and information officers in a holiday area or taxi drivers in London. A wine bar which opened in Covent Garden invited taxi drivers to an opening breakfast so that they would know where it was. Other people whom it may be politic to ask to any kind of opening function are your immediate neighbours. These are the people who could cause trouble if your customers have problems parking or get a little noisy on occasion. If you are on good terms with them they are likely to be a little more tolerant than if you ignore them.

Such activities come under the general heading of public relations and it is well worth keeping in contact with all the people who may be able to pass on information to a wider public.

On the whole it is not really worth investing a lot of time and money on advertising and promotion once you have got the launch safely past, but you will want to publicise special events, live entertainers, wine tastings and the like. An advertisement on the entertainments page of the local paper will be useful, but in addition to this, don't overlook posters and don't forget to post information in the bar too.

Keeping up the standards

Special events advertising and good public relations are all useful tools but by far the most valuable recommendation that any establishment can have is by word of mouth from satisfied customers. Your own high standard of food and wine and service will be the best public relations help you can have.

Indeed, the one piece of advice which was common to all the wine bar owners I have interviewed could be summed up as, 'Identify a standard right at the start and keep it up.' This standard must apply to all aspects of the bar's activities and to the customers as well.

The proprietor of a wine bar is at liberty to refuse to serve anyone he chooses, nor does he have to give a reason for such a refusal, though it is probably sensible to do so. Many owners use this right to ensure that the clientele live up to the standards expected of them. If a customer is banned for violent behaviour then this ban can be upheld in the courts, as the licensee is responsible for keeping proper order. This right covers offensive dress or behaviour.

Age limit

The wine bar owner must not knowingly sell intoxicating liquor to a person under 18 or knowingly allow any other person to do so nor allow a person under 18 to consume intoxicating liquor in a bar.

Children under 14 are not allowed in a bar licensed mainly for the use and sale of intoxicating liquor, but children will be allowed in a wine bar which has only a restaurant licence or in a bar which has an area used only for meals and where the sale or supply of intoxicating liquor is only to people having such meals.

Tobacco may not be sold to persons under the

age of 16 years. The licence to sell intoxicating liquor also authorises the sale of tobacco.

Remember, your reputation is at stake

Start by checking on yourself. It is very easy to let things slip a little when you are very busy. Are you as genuinely welcoming as you were when the wine bar first opened? Do you take time out to talk to as many customers as possible both to explain and recommend items off the wine list and menu and to listen to their comments? Are you, in fact, setting a good example to the staff?

Next look at your staff, asking some of the same questions and checking that the service offered is as good as it can be. Remember that really good service is rare these days and so ready and willing service can be a promotional tool in its own right.

The wine list and the menu are the next areas for review. Are they still as carefully worked out as they were when you opened? Are all the systems operating smoothly and correctly, or have you lost sight of the goal you had in the beginning? This can happen almost without your noticing it.

A wine bar owner in the Midlands suddenly realised that his clientele was starting to change. Large numbers of young people had started to come in the evening and use the wine bar rather like a pub. This meant that the regular evening wine drinkers and many of the diners were beginning to stay away. Drastic action was called for and the proprietor placed an advertisement in the local paper and in the bar stating that no one would be served a drink without food. He also removed the one beer pump. After a few days of enforcing the new rule the youngsters went elsewhere and the regular clientele started to return. In due course the rule was allowed to lapse and small supplies of bottled beer were kept to supply the occasional request for beer.

On the whole, high standards in the running of a bar encourage equally high standards from the customer but the customer must know what is exepcted of him. A wine bar in one of the university towns makes it quite clear to students that, although they are welcome, they are expected to behave and on the whole there is very little trouble.

It is important to nip in the bud any problems before they develop. If you do not, you may have to resort to the actions described above and might not be so lucky in getting all your original customers back. Some customers will try it on, particularly if the bar is new and they don't know you. 'Just another quick one,' or 'Just a few more minutes while we finish our discussions,' are common enough pleas but you must stand firm. Do not set any precedents and treat everyone the same.

On the other hand, you may get complaints about the food or the wine; here it is not the law but your standards that are being called into question and your response should be much more yielding. Wine bars with the highest standards always consider the customer to be in the right even when he is not!

Appendix

Further reading

An ABC of the Licensing Law, National Union of Licensed Victuallers, Boardman House, 2 Downing Street, Farnham, Surrey

An A-Z of Employment and Safety Law, Peter Chandler (Kogan Page)

Consumer Law for the Small Business, Patricia Clayton (Kogan Page)

Croner's Reference Book for the Self-employed and Smaller Business (Croner Publications)

Guardian Guide to Running a Small Business, The, 3rd edn, ed Clive Woodcock (Kogan Page)

How to Buy a Business, Peter Farrell (Kogan Page)

Law for the Small Business, The Daily Telegraph Guide, 3rd edn, Patricia Clayton (Kogan Page)

Raising Finance: the Guardian Guide for the Small Business, Clive Woodcock (Kogan Page)

Small Business Guide, The, Colin Barrow (BBC Publications)

Sunday Telegraph Good Wine Guide, published annually

Understand Your Accounts, A St J Price (Kogan Page)

Which? Wine Guide, published annually by the Consumers' Association (Hodder & Stoughton)

The Wine Drinkers Handbook, Serena Sutcliffe (Pan Books)

Working for Yourself: the Daily Telegraph Guide to Self-employment, 6th edn, Godfrey Golzen (Kogan Page)

The World Atlas of Wine, 19th edn, Hugh Johnson (Mitchell Beazley)

Journals

Catering, 161–5 Greenwich House, Greenwich High Street, London SE10 8JA

Catering and Hotel Management, Link House, Dingwell Avenue, Croydon, Surrey CR9 2AT

Catering Times, Quadrant House, The Quadrant, Sutton, Surrey SM2 5AS

Decanter, 16 Blackfriars Lane, London EC4V 6EB

Drinks Marketing, 100 Fleet Street, London EC4B 4LA

Harpers Wine and Spirit Trade Gazette, Harling House, 47–51 Great Suffolk Street, London SE1 0BS

The Publican, Maclaren House, 19 Scarbrook Road, Croydon, Surrey CR9 1QH

Wine and Spirit, 38–42 Hampton Road, Teddington, Middlesex TW11 0JE

Winepress, 16 Ennismore Avenue, London W4 15F

Which? Wine Monthly, Consumers' Association, 14 Buckingham Street, London WC2N 6DS

Useful addresses

National telephone dialling codes are given, though local codes may differ.

Local councils and Chambers of Commerce can be good sources of help and information. Many organisations listed below will have local offices.

Advisory, Conciliation and Arbitration Service (ACAS)

Head Office, Cleland House, Page Street, London SW1P 4ND; 01-222 8020.

Alliance of Small Firms and Self-Employed People
42 Vine Road, East Molesey, Surrey KT8 9LF; 01-979 2293

British Insurance Brokers Association
Fountain House, 130 Fenchurch Street, London EC3M 5DJ; 01-623 9043

Council for Small Industries in Rural Areas (CoSIRA)
141 Castle Street, Salisbury, Wiltshire SP1 3TP; 0722 6255

Department of Industry, Small Firms Division
Ashdown House, 127 Victoria Street, London SW1E 6RB; 01-212 8667, 8721, 6206

Freefone 2444 for all regional offices listed below:

London and South Eastern Region
Ebury Bridge House, 2–18 Ebury Bridge Road, London SW1W 8QD

South Western Region
5th Floor, The Pithay, Bristol BS1 2NB

Northern Region
22 Newgate Shopping Centre, Newcastle upon Tyne NE1 3EE

North West Region
320–25 Royal Exchange Buildings, St Ann's Square, Manchester M2 7AH
1 Old Hall Street, Liverpool L3 9HJ

Yorkshire and Humberside Region
1 Park Row, City Square, Leeds LS1 5NR

East Midlands Region
48–50 Maid Marian Way, Nottingham NG1 6GF

West Midlands Region
Ladywood House, Stephenson Street, Birmingham B2 4DT

Eastern Region
24 Brooklands Avenue, Cambridge CB2 2BU

Dolamore Ltd
15 Craven Road, London W2; 01-723 8894

Peter Dominic Ltd
Vintner House, River Way, Harlow, Essex; 0279 26391

English Vineyards Association
The Ridge, Lamberhurst Down, Kent TN3 8ER

Food and Wine from France
Nuffield House, 41–6 Piccadilly, London W1V 9AJ; 01-439 8371

German Food Centre
44 Knightsbridge, London SW1X 7SN; 01-235 5760

German Wine Information Service
121 Gloucester Place, London W1H 3PJ; 01-935 8164

Glass Manufacturers' Federation
Environmental Officer, 19 Portland Place, London W1N 4BH; 01-580 6952

Grants of St James
Eastgate House, 10 Nottingham Road, Derby DE1 3TB; 0332 31201

Hallgarten Wines
53 Carkers Lane, Highgate Road, London NW5 1RR; 01-267 5932

Health and Safety Commission
Regina House, 259 Old Marylebone Road, London NW1 5RR; 01-723 1262

Health and Safety Executive
25 Chapel Street, London NW1 5DT; 01-262 3277

HM Customs and Excise
VAT Administration Directorate, King's Beam House, Mark Lane, London EC3R 7HE; 01-283 8911

Industrial and Commercial Finance Corporation (ICFC)
91 Waterloo Road, London SE1 8XP; 01-928 7822

The Kenco Coffee Company Ltd
Strathville Road, London SW18 4QY; 01-874 6191

London Enterprise Agency (LEntA)
69 Cannon Street, London EC4N 5AB; 01-236 2676

The Nairobi Coffee and Tea Company
Shakespeare Street, Industrial Estate, Watford WD2 5HF; 0923 34561

Northern Ireland Development Agency
Maryfield, 100 Belfast Road, Hollywood, County Down
Local Enterprise Development Unit
Lamont House, Purdy's Lane, Newtownbreda, Belfast BT8 4AR; 0232 691031
Performing Rights Society Ltd
29 Berners Street, London W1A 4PP; 01-580 5544
Phonographic Performance Ltd
Ganton House, 14 Ganton Street, London W1B 1LB; 01-437 0311
Registrar of Companies
Companies House, Crown Way, Maindy, Cardiff CF4 3UZ; 0222 388588
102 George Street, Edinburgh EH2 3DJ; 031-225 5774
43-7 Chichester Street, Belfast BT1 4RJ; 0232 234121
Reynier Ltd
16-18 Upper Tachbrook Street, London SW1V 1SL; 01-834 2917
Scottish Development Agency
120 Bothwell Street, Glasgow G2 7JP; 041-248 2700
102 Telford Road, Edinburgh EH4 2NP; 031-343 1911
Stowells of Chelsea
Priorswell Road, Worksop, Nottinghamshire S80 2BZ; 0909 474661
Victoria Wines
Brook House, Chertsey Road, Woking, Surrey GU21 5BE; 04862 5066
Vinos de España
22-3 Manchester Square, London W1M 5AP; 01-935 6140
Welsh Development Agency
Treforest Industrial Estate, Pontypridd, Mid Glamorgan CF37 5UT; 0443 852666
The Wine Standards Board
Wine Inspectorate, $68\frac{1}{2}$ Upper Thames Street, London EC4V 3BJ; 01-236 9512

Index